owl

The Disintegration of
the Monolith

The Disintegration of the Monolith

BORIS KAGARLITSKY

Translated by
Renfrey Clarke

VERSO
London · New York

First published by Verso 1992
© Verso 1992
All rights reserved

Verso
UK: 6 Meard Street, London W1V 3HR
USA: 29 West 35th Street, New York, NY 10001-2291

Verso is the imprint of New Left Books

ISBN 0-86091-363-5
ISBN 0-86091-573-5 (pbk)

British Library Cataloguing in Publication Data
A catalogue record for this book is available from the British Library

Library of Congress Cataloging-in-Publication Data
A catalogue record for this book is available from the Library of Congress

Typeset by York House Typographic Ltd, London W7
Printed in Great Britain by Biddles Ltd, Guildford and Kings Lynn

Contents

Foreword   vii

Introduction   1

1 The Heirs of Totalitarianism   9

2 Intellectuals versus the Intelligentsia: A Crisis of Culture   30

3 Political Mosaic: Left and Right   45

4 A New Model of Democracy? Populism   61

5 Pluralism Russian Style: A Multiplicity of Good Parties?   77

6 Is There an Alternative? The Market, but What Kind of Market?   94

7 Totalitarianism: The Return of the Repressed   104

8 The Time for Repentance   113

9 The Coup that Worked   133

10 Winter of Discontent   139

11 Russia on the Brink of New Battles   157

Foreword

During the years of Gorbachev's rule, Soviet society was in a chronic state of crisis and collapse. The ruling circles not only learnt how to live quite happily in crisis conditions but even began to derive benefit from them, profiting from the country's ruin, selling off national property to foreigners, looting and 'privatizing' everything valuable and viable that still remained.

Meanwhile, the crisis entered a new phase. The Union of Soviet Socialist Republics, formed by the Bolsheviks in 1922 to consolidate the gains of their revolution, disintegrated in December 1991, a few days before its seventieth anniversary. Amid the clamour about the triumph of liberty and the eradication of communism, the country simply fell apart. The liquidation of the Union has not solved a single national conflict nor has it altered the imperial essence of the state. All of the former Soviet republics proclaiming the foundation of the Commonwealth of Independent States are structurally mini-empires. They contain the same inherent contradictions as the large Union. At the helm stand local leaders, who as a rule have come to power through semi-free elections and the manipulation of public opinion. Not one of the former Soviet republics constituting the Commonwealth possesses normally functioning democratic institutions. The law is frequently disregarded and the rulers treat the state as if it were their own property.

The borders of the republics, arbitrarily drawn by Stalin's bureaucrats, cannot be stable, economic independence is a myth and even the Commonwealth's common market remains only a good idea. All who are able to are arming themselves and trying to defend themselves against each other. All the regional overlords are striving to create their own army, if possible with nuclear weapons, their own currency, and their own ambassadors at foreign courts. At a local level, petty leaders are endeavouring to win the same rights for themselves. In Georgia, the elected, if autocratic, president has been overthrown by the armed forces and Shevardnadze, the former boss of Soviet Georgia, installed in his place. The Chechen republic is striving for independence from Russia and in the Crimea the demand for independence from the Ukraine has been raised.

Hobbes once characterized the feudal-barbarian society which existed in the West prior to the triumph of the absolutist nation state as 'the war of all against all'. This definition is now ideally suited to the society which the ex-Soviet Union has become. In essence, the empire has broken up not into nation states but into feudal domains and princedoms. Having gained in strength, the local lords rushed to get rid of the supreme ruler. The emperor himself worried them more than the formal preservation of the empire. Gorbachev's personal involvement in the political life of the republics was still a serious political problem despite the fact that, after the August 1991 putsch, Yeltsin had in fact liquidated the Union's institutions of government in Russia and made Gorbachev his hostage on the pretext of the struggle against the USSR president's comrades, who had attempted to declare a state of emergency.

The decision taken by the princes, gathered in the government dacha in Belovezhsky forest, essentially affected Gorbachev alone. The presidency was abolished. No president, no country. No Gorbachev, no USSR. The president resigned and the red flag was taken down from the Kremlin. In other words, they removed the emperor's personal standard from the castle and raised the prince's banner.

In the West, the end of Gorbachev has been called the end of perestroika. In fact, perestroika as an attempt at purposeful reform ended back in 1990 when the powers of the Union and the republics, realizing that they could not halt the slide into crisis, began to adapt to the situation and exploit it in their own interests.

Now the time has come for 'economic reform'. Over the course of several years, reforms have been prepared, proclaimed and discussed. But no one could bring him or herself to assume responsibility for their practical implementation since those holding power understood that it was not simply a question of lowering the people's living standards but of a genuine social and economic catastrophe, of turning an averagely developed, independent, industrial country experiencing difficulties into a poorly developed one, into a semi-colony, into the economic periphery of the West.

However, many political figures and entrepreneurs are already finding that the destruction of their country is a highly profitable affair.

Those who had long supported Gorbachev and then, having thrown him away like a poor hand of cards, brought Yeltsin to power, can now finally enjoy the fruits of their success. Everything that can be divided up, pulled apart or plundered will be privatized and distributed among the top people in the state. Anything which does not reach the top will go to the hangers-on. The remainder will be picked up by the mafia which, as the liberal press has already announced, 'does not exist in our country'.

Having captured Rome, the barbarians began to construct their own crooked and unprepossessing buildings, pilfering stones from the Colosseum and the grandiose edifices of the empire. Sometimes they would try to start building from the top, and sometimes they would pull down a column and the roof would fall on someone's head. The economy of the former USSR is being reconstructed in much the same way.

Our empire, like any other, deserved to crash, but its heirs are a new breed of barbarians. Having announced the return to the bosom of world civilization, they are undermining the elementary foundations of civilized life itself without any thought for the consequences, pulling down the education system, destroying the nursery system (incidentally, for all its shortcomings, generally acknowledged to be the best in the world) and, while incapable of nurturing the private entrepreneur, liquidating the state sector of the economy, the only means at present of ensuring the mass production of the cheap goods needed by society.

We were promised capitalism and we have got it. The ordinary people and the hordes of leaders all envisaged the rich displays of the best Paris shops, forgetting about the half-starved unemployed of Lima and São Paulo. The plane has taken off and a section of the public still believes it will land in Paris or Stockholm. But, in fact, the course has been set for Brazil, or even Nigeria, since this airline and this make of plane do not fly to the West at all. True, some will achieve their aim and live in Moscow as if it were Paris – but at the expense of those who will live as if in South America or Africa.

The West has supposedly decided to grant generous aid to Yeltsin in his heroic endeavour to bury the Soviet Pact and build a glorious capitalist future. Yet somehow even the modest amount agreed, no more than $24 billion, is to be paid over a period of years. It is to be used to support the currency and to maintain service payments on debts to Western institutions. And even these sums are only forthcoming so long as the Moscow government meekly allows its policies to be dictated from abroad, and permits Russia's resources to be bought at knockdown prices by Western companies. No wonder Yeltsin was well received in Washington, as was Gorbachev before him. Yet Western commentators should ponder the fate of their previous favourite.

It's easy to guess how this might all end. The barbarism of those at the top provokes protest from those at the bottom, but God forbid that this protest should prove as barbaric as the policies which engendered it. The politicians of the new intake are already awaiting their moment. If anyone thought that by liquidating the Communist Party of the Soviet Union (CPSU) they were eliminating Communist ideology, they were profoundly mistaken. New parties are taking the place of the corrupt and bureaucratized CPSU. Their leaders are, as a rule, sincere. They won't speculate in diamonds like Gorbachev's Politburo. They believe in what they say and won't change their opinions every month.

The most active of the new parties is the Russian Communist Workers' Party. Alongside them stands the party of Bolsheviks headed by Nina Andreeva. Apart from them are smaller and more moderate groups comprising members of the old apparatus who were not picked up by the Russian government. These are assembled under the banner of the Socialist Workers' Party, which, however, having united the 'Gorbachevites without Gorbachev', is so anxious to look respectable that it has already earned the reputation of being an 'exceptionally boring party'.

The strength of Communist movements always lay in the fact that they told the truth about workers' exploitation and lack of rights. But the cure they proposed always proved worse than the illness. We need no further examples to be convinced of that.

A modern left-wing organization which has broken with the traditions of barracks communism can become the alternative to barbarism triumphant under the slogans of privatization and 'liberalization'. Today in Moscow, St Petersburg, Irkutsk and the Urals, the Party of Labour has united the majority of the left-wing groups which came into existence during the years of perestroika, and is expanding its activity. It gives some hope that sooner or later in our country another politics will become possible, not the politics of leaders and princes, but the politics of the masses, the politics of social interests. Perhaps then our choice will not be limited to different versions of barbarism.

May 1992

Introduction

Few can doubt that extraordinary changes have taken place in the former Soviet Union. The old and new authorities have helpfully staged some episodes of high drama to impress this fact on us. We have seen tanks in the streets of Moscow, coups have been proclaimed by one group and then taken over by another, the Congress of People's Deputies has wound itself up and new independent republics have been proclaimed. MacDonalds has opened for business, the statue of Dzerzhinsky in front of the KGB headquarters has been dismantled, the Soviet flag has been hauled down and that of the Russian Republic flutters in its place over the Kremlin. Moscow's Arbat now contains a continuous street market. The former ruling Communist Party and its property have been seized. The bemused peoples of the former USSR were told that they belonged to the Union of Sovereign States which was then rapidly replaced by the Community or Commonwealth of Independent States (CIS). They were also treated to lengthy lectures on economic reform, which they were told must mean stiff price rises and wholesale privatization. But while they could hardly complain of lack of incident perhaps less was changing than appeared to be the case, and perhaps the real changes do not have their source in the liberal coup of August 1991 but stem from the whole period of perestroika and indeed the epoch which preceded it. In the street markets which have been springing up since the late 1980s the stalls did a brisk trade in *matrushka*, Russian dolls painted to look like Gorbachev, inside whom was to be found Brezhnev, then Stalin, then Lenin. Following the coup of August 1991 the street stalls were quickly supplied with Yeltsin dolls, with Russia's president draped in the national flag, inside whom were Gorbachev and his predecessors. The conclusion that everything is changing only to stay the same tells us only part of the story. There have been changes but they are not what they are claimed to be. Thus in most former Soviet republics the new anti-communist authorities bear a striking resemblance to the old Communist order but the change in official rhetoric is not just empty. While we do not have the consumer capitalism we have been promised, the beginnings of another sort of capitalism are visible enough.

In Moscow in the late autumn or winter of 1988 I met with a British parliamentary delegation, most of whose members, naturally, were Conservatives. The conversation turned to perestroika, and to meetings which had been organized for the foreign guests with official Soviet experts. 'I'm a convinced supporter of Mrs Thatcher,' said one of the visitors, 'and I've always strongly defended the market. But what your economists are saying is absolutely preposterous! They think the economy can function without any regulation whatever, that you can simply abolish subsidies to agriculture. They completely fail to understand how appalling the results of such a policy could be. No British Conservative would ever agree to it.'

The absurdity of the situation lay not so much in the fact that this visitor, who in his own country gave consistent backing to the free market, should have appeared to us in Moscow to be a supporter of state regulation, as in the fact that the experts whom he had met in the Soviet Union, as it then was, were by no means our most extreme liberals. He was referring to official experts working for the Communist Party, people whom the leaders of our liberal intelligentsia were then constantly accusing of inconsistency, of indecisiveness, of an inability to stand firmly behind the positions of the market.

The final collapse of communism in the Soviet Union was preceded by the rapid dissemination of liberal ideology within the old ruling strata, the enumeration of the advantages of capitalism in official Communist publications, the sharp rightward turn of well-known figures in the democratic opposition who not long before had been proclaiming their devotion to the values of socialism or who had even held Marxist views. Naturally such developments, culminating in the hauling down of the red flag and the break-up of the old Union, could not fail to arouse enthusiasm among Western right-wingers.

A sign of the times was a statement by the American philosopher Francis Fukuyama. In the autumn of 1989 he informed the world, in an article much bruited in the Western media, that 'history has come to an end'. The final event in history had been the universal triumph of capitalism and liberal democracy on the Western model. 'Marxism–Leninism' had been the final attempt to advance an ideology and construct a system representing an alternative to liberalism. This attempt had suffered a definitive failure, and the universal affirmation of liberalism now represented the only possible future for humanity.

Fukuyama even complained that in future life would be dull. From his sublime eminence as possessor of the final, incontrovertible scientific truth he delivered his judgement that Hegel, who had predicted the end of history, was correct, and all subsequent philosophers had strayed from the true path.

It goes without saying that such reasoning could never be taken seriously in a scientific argument. But ideological nonsense differs from the more usual type precisely because it reflects a particular trend of thought. And indeed, Fukuyama's arguments have had a noticeable resonance not only among right-wingers but also among leftists. *Marxism Today*, the journal of the British Communist Party, launched an extensive discussion of Fukuyama's ideas and the Labourite journal *New Socialist* also joined in. Most curious of all, it became clear that on the major questions under debate the views of many 'left' opponents of liberalism did not differ significantly from those of Fukuyama. This is not only true of Britain. The demoralization and deideologization of the left that were sharply exacerbated by events in the 'Eastern' bloc at the end of the 1980s is now a characteristic tendency in most Western countries. A glance through Italian and French journals that have traditionally expressed the views of left-wing intellectuals shows that by 1988–89 the discussion on how to overcome capitalism had changed to thoughts on how best to adapt to it.

Nevertheless this 'triumph of capitalism', like many other ideological triumphs, has turned out to be premature. Instead of being integrated into a 'free and prosperous Europe', the former Communist countries have encountered growing difficulties, and within a few months of the conquest of democratic liberties talk began to be heard everywhere about the danger of new dictatorships. Public subsidies for essential items of popular consumption were ended; but, to show evenhandedness, so were subsidies to cultural and educational bodies like theatre groups, orchestras, publishing houses and research institutes. Hundreds of thousands were thrown into unemployment, millions on short-time work expected to follow them. The turn-out for elections began to drop below 50 per cent. For many people in Eastern Europe this encounter with the realities of the capitalist market was an unpleasant surprise. The American journal *The Nation* asked:

What will happen if the world experiences another severe economic downturn like the one in the mid-1970s, or an even more severe crisis on the scale of the Great Depression? What a disappointment would be in store for millions of people in Eastern Europe, if their faith in the God-Market were to suffer the same crash as their faith in the God-Party.[1]

Meanwhile, the Western economies in the 1990s can no longer guarantee the steady growth seen throughout most of the preceding decades. The fat years are turning into lean ones.

Many people in the Eastern bloc have believed devoutly in the myth of wealthy, democratic capitalist society, without knowing or wanting to know the truth about the impoverishment of the Third World, about the hunger and deprivation of the majority of people who live under real capitalism. This has an exact parallel in the way Communists did not know, or did not want to know, the truth about the Stalinist prison camps, about repression and economic mismanagement in the then USSR. Those who held illusions then are now being made to pay for them. Western Communists and other leftists are paying through a crisis of confidence, through demoralization, through a loss of values. It is as though Communists were soon to be consigned to the 'Red Book' (not, of course, the little red book of Chairman Mao, which despite being printed in millions of copies has long since become a rarity to be sought in antiquarian bookshops, but the real 'Red Book' which lists extinct species – the marsupial wolf, the Ussuri tiger and other exotic creatures).

In Eastern Europe events have unfolded with special rapidity. During the autumn of 1989 the Communist parties were not only driven from power but in the majority of countries they simply disappeared. They dissolved themselves, changed their names along with their leadership, organizational forms and programmes, or simply fell apart. The picture in the West was not much brighter. The Communist Party of Italy, the most popular and influential of all the Western Communist parties, an organization with a long democratic tradition, the progenitor of 'Eurocommunism', was the first to raise the question of liquidation. In its place a democratic left party was formed, with a completely new programme and organizational structures. It was hoped that the composition of the party would change, attracting those leftists who traditionally had been opposed to the Communist movement. But in fact this move led to a damaging split in which the newly formed Democratic Left Party found itself in a weaker position than before.

Nevertheless the Italian Communists provided an example to others. The Communist Party of Finland disbanded. A Union of Left Forces was established, a completely new organization which came together from the grassroots. The Swedish 'Left Party – Communists' also dropped the communist label, becoming simply the 'Left Party' and renouncing its old programme. The Communist Party of the Netherlands ceased to exist as a separate body, joining with the Socialists and Greens in a party of the 'Green Lefts'.

The process has not been confined to Europe. For several years now there has been no Communist Party in Mexico. In the summer of 1990 the Canadian Communists decided to change their name, purging their programme of all references to Marxism–Leninism and deleting democratic centralism from their statutes. This was not a 'Eurocommunist' party which had long been following this road, but a thoroughly orthodox Stalinist-Brezhnevite organization. It seems, however, that the change came too late; the party's rank-and-file members and supporters scattered in all directions. The party's meetings and public functions began to attract only a third to a half as many people as two years previously. 'I don't want to be identified with Nicolae Ceausescu,' party leader George Hewson laments, 'and I don't think anyone in our party wants that.'[2]

The Communist Party of the USA, traditionally a loyal ally of the CPSU, has fallen on hard times. Supporters of renewal attack the old leadership, and Brezhnev supporter Gus Hall threatens to use administrative measures against the heretics:

> How should the party deal with a member of the National Committee, who in a radio broadcast replies to a question on whether the CPUSA has drawn any lessons from events in Eastern Europe by saying, 'We need to purge the party of Stalinism and Stalinist leaders.' If it's me they were talking about, then it's an irresponsible slander![3]

What needs to be done? Rank-and-file Communist Party members themselves are now becoming convinced that as a result of events in the USSR and Eastern Europe, 'the majority of people will find the word "communism" repellent for many years to come'.[4]

It is not simply a matter of words. One can, after all, change the sign but not the shop. The genuine causes of the crisis lie much deeper. The Communist parties, founded at the beginning of the century on the basis of strict organizational and ideological discipline, implementing their political line through a centralized apparatus, identifying socialism with an all-powerful state and regarding themselves as the sole vanguard of the working class and of humanity in general, were ill-fitted to the conditions of a new, complex and dynamic world. With their outmoded methods they were unable to defend the interests of the workers even in such countries as Italy and Finland, where they traditionally enjoyed prestige as serious popular, democratic forces.

The transformation they have been forced to carry through in order to keep up with changing circumstances was too great: so great, in fact, as to pose the question: what, if anything, is going to remain?

In the contemporary world, where the computer coexists with the spade, and where the countries of Eastern Europe in the space of two months are transformed from colonies of Moscow's empire into the periphery of the West, even small parties that are based on traditional Communist principles are revealed as clumsy and backward. This has also been true of the Trotskyist parties, which have nowhere succeeded in profiting from the crisis of communism, despite their often much more attractive names ('Workers League', 'Proletarian Democracy', 'Socialist Outlook', etc.). Even the Social Democrats, who have always condemned communism but who are organized on much the same principles, are undergoing a crisis, and are losing one position after another in the developed industrial countries.

In this the supporters of liberal capitalism see clear evidence of a worldwide decline of the forces of the left, which is supposed to prove the bankruptcy not only of communism, but also of socialist ideas. Nevertheless, the most diverse countries are now witnessing the rapid growth of new left–socialist parties which reject centralist organizational forms and dogmatic ideology. The Socialist Left Party in Norway and the Socialist People's Party in Denmark have strongly increased their representation in parliament, placing heavy pressure on the Social Democrats. Popular support for the Swedish Left Party has doubled since it rid itself of the spectre of communism by changing its programme and reviewing its organizational structure. The same is happening with the Brazilian Workers Party, the Dutch Green Lefts, the Spanish United Lefts and so on.

The new socialists strive to combine the ideas of economic decentralization and environmental priorities with the left's traditional demands for social justice. They criticize the capitalist market, defending self-management and democratically organized, socially controlled forms of collective property, while rejecting the idea of total statization. They are proving an attractive alternative for voters.

But all this is happening 'over there'.

The CPSU did everything it could to maintain its glory as the last Communist Party in Europe. So long as it still had millions of members, so long as its bureaucrats received their wages, so long as the party remained the owner of buildings, newspapers and bank accounts, it was possible for members to console themselves with the illusion that despite 'certain difficulties' and 'the complexity of the political conjuncture', on the whole everything was under control.

Unfortunately, experience had already shown repeatedly that mere material strength was not enough. Being a big party and a rich party did not necessarily mean being a strong party, the more so since anti-communist attitudes were growing in society. The crowds who gathered at street meetings were not the only ones shouting anti-communist slogans. Even before the events of August 1991 brought about the collapse and dissolution of the Communist Party, the president of the Leningrad Soviet, Anatoly Sobchak, had called in an interview with the journal *Ogonyok* for the Communist Party to be outlawed. In the Soviet constitution, which these very Communists had approved, the juridical basis for such a prohibition already existed. Our constitution was the only one in the world which prohibited not only the propaganda of the national enemy but also the dissemination of the ideas of the social one. It is not hard to guess who this clause of the constitution was directed against.

It was enough to watch television or glance through the local youth newspapers, let alone *Ogonyok* or *Kommersant*, to grasp that anti-communism was little by little becoming part of the ruling ideology. There was nothing good about this; anti-communism was the mirror image of totalitarian intolerance and its direct successor. Something else was clear as well: through its past and present policies the CPSU had prepared the ground for anti-communism, nourishing the anti-communists and giving rise to an ideological context in which calls for a new dictatorship, this time directed at the eradication of the red menace, were coming to appear natural.

The CPSU functionaries hoped to find a way out of their ideological impasse through borrowing alien ideas. While party documents echoed the demands of the liberals for privatization and a free market, they never failed to remind the reader of environmental dangers, and repeated the slogans advanced by the supporters of self-management. One found phrases about alienation, borrowings from the works of Western Marxists of the 'revisionist' school, and promises to preserve social guarantees during the transition to the market, at the same time as these guarantees were being undermined by the policies of the Communist-led government.

This hotchpotch cooked up out of scraps of alien phraseology was no substitute for a distinct political identity. But the CPSU no longer had a face of its own. The party tried to take its distance from the past, belatedly and inconsistently. But from what sources could it renew itself? And how in these circumstances could the party remain communist, how could it preserve its continuity with that previous party, the party of Stalin, Khrushchev and Brezhnev, which sent large numbers of its own founders to the firing squad? Could the party return to Lenin? To Trotsky? To Bukharin? Return to 1917 or 1922? And should it return to the past, even to the age of revolutionary glory?

Only the utterly naïve could hope that the massive defection of rank-and-file members and high-placed functionaries from the CPSU would bring about a return to health, with the uncommitted leaving and the true Communists remaining. As its membership shrank, the party remained just as heterogeneous. And in any case, what does it mean to be a 'true Communist' at the end of the twentieth century?

The Communist movement has come to its logical end. But this is not the end of socialism, for the simple reason that with every day that passes capitalism shows itself less and less capable of solving the problems of our epoch. Having triumphed in the ideological struggle with communism, capitalism has run up against its own self, its own contradictions and difficulties. In this sense Eastern Europe, having shown the world the non-viability of the Communist project, is now, it seems, doomed to experience the collapse of yet another experiment, this time a liberal one. If the triumph of capitalism has turned out to be premature, then reports of the death of socialism are, as the saying goes, much exaggerated.

The well-known political scientist B. P. Kurashvili wrote:

> In the words of a bitter joke, history has nothing left to inflict on us, when twenty-five years of terror are followed by ten years of fuss, and twenty years of stagnation turn into five years of collapse. But no – Soviet history is richer, its weighty dramas cleanse and instruct us. . . .[5]

All of this is forcing us to seek a new path, to discuss a new democratic and socialist alternative. And this new struggle is still only beginning.

Notes

1. *The Nation*, 1990, vol. 251, 4, p. 127
2. *Toronto Star*, 12 April 1990.
3. *Workers Vanguard*, 1 June 1990.
4. *Canadian Tribune*, 7 May 1990.
5. B. P. Kurashvili, *Strana na rasput'e* ('The Country at the Crossroads'), Moscow 1990.

1

The Heirs of Totalitarianism

Stalinism

The changes which began in the Soviet Union and Eastern Europe at the end of the 1980s astonished foreign observers (and often the participants themselves) with their rapidity. The system of totalitarian power which had proved its resilience over the decades and had endured numerous shocks during the 1950s and 1960s unexpectedly crumbled into dust. In its place arose a new society, unfamiliar even to those who lived within it.

In actual fact, the precipitate nature of the changes was the consequence of a natural process of evolution which had taken place over many years in the depths of the system itself. Throughout the 1970s partial shifts in the structure of society gradually accumulated, preparing the way for the crisis which was to follow. At the end of the 1980s these changes burst on to the scene. Quantity had become quality.

The 'classic' totalitarian regime was installed in the Soviet Union at the beginning of the 1930s, when the private sector in the towns was finally liquidated, independent peasant property was expropriated, the rural population was herded together in co-operative farms, the opposition groups within the party were finally crushed, and a system of central planning was substituted for an economy which combined state regulation with the operation of the market. These new relationships, however, did not arise out of a vacuum.

The revolution of 1917, like all revolutions, voiced the slogans of social liberation, while at the same time the new regime was confronted with the task of modernizing the country. The inability of the Tsarist regime and the Russian bourgeoisie to carry out rapid modernization had led to catastrophic defeats in the war against Japan in 1904 and 1905 and in the First World War. Capitalist industrialization had not only established large industrial enterprises in Russia, but had also

9

ogical visible.

given birth to all the contradictions characteristic of early industrial society at the end of the nineteenth and beginning of the twentieth centuries. At the same time, it had not ensured a dynamic process of development enabling Russia to stand on the same level as the West. A proletariat and a social democratic movement appeared, but the ruling classes, unlike those of the West, had neither the resources nor the experience to prevent a social explosion through the use of compromises, rises in the standard of living, and partial satisfaction of the demands emerging from below.

The task of modernization, which had not been carried out by the old regime, was passed on to the new. The future of the new authorities now depended on their ability to carry through this transformation.

The shifting of power from the soviets to the Bolshevik party, the installation during the Civil War of a one-party dictatorship, the subordination of the trade unions to the state, and the gradual consolidation of an authoritarian regime within the party itself signified that the revolution had completely lost not only its democratic but also its socialist character. The working class, which was still cited as the ruling power, and which to a certain degree still formed the social base of the regime, became subordinated to a new party-state bureaucracy which had coalesced within the revolutionary movement.

Socialist and Marxist theoreticians reacted with bewilderment to the new state, which had grown out of the revolution but which was tragically unlike what they had expected. Leon Trotsky wrote:

The poverty and cultural backwardness of the masses were once again embodied in the sinister figure of the overseer with a big stick in his hands. From being the servant of society, the bureaucracy that was the object of so many complaints and curses has once again become its master. Through this process the bureaucracy has suffered such a degree of social and moral alienation from the popular masses that it can no longer allow the masses to exercise the slightest control either over its actions or its incomes.[1]

Drawing an analogy with the French Revolution, Trotsky termed this the 'Soviet Thermidor', And there is indeed a similarity, for post-revolutionary society passed through the same phases in the Soviet Union as in France, though the forms and time-frames were different. The 'Thermidorean' regime of the bureaucratic heirs of the revolution gradually assumed an imperialist character, took to expanding through military force, enslaved neighbouring countries and installed regimes there which were organized on the model and in the image of Big Brother. The decay in turn of the imperial system, both in our case and

that of France, has involved a partial restoration of the old pre-
revolutionary relationships, but on a basis of respect for the rights and
property of the new ruling elite which arose as a result of the revolution. In this sense perestroika has turned out to be a kind of analogue in
Russian history of the restoration of the Bourbons in France.

Moreover, it is quite clear that the ruling groups could not, either
then or now, carry out reforms without finally renouncing the rem-
nants of their revolutionary ideology. The Stalinist Thermidor, like that
in France, was in essence a counterrevolution spawned by the revolution itself and to a significant degree forming the continuation and
culmination of the revolution. Therefore, attempts to separate Bolshevism from Stalinism and attempts to treat Bolshevism as the progenitor
of Stalinism are equally absurd. It follows that when the regime, which
had made skilled use of the revolutionary heritage to provide an
ideological justification for its rule, eventually sought to cast off this
heritage, it could not do so. Promises to pursue a 'non-capitalist' path
were still essential for maintaining the political stability of the system,
even if everything in the regime's practice contradicted this slogan.

Although the Soviet regime's socialist perspectives had been
exhausted, and although the class nature of its power had gradually
been changing, this did not in the least signify a rejection of the policy
of modernizing the country. Indeed, the modernization and industrialization of Russia henceforth became the regime's central tasks. From
this point the 'construction of socialism' was presented mainly as the
construction of a large array of up-to-date industrial enterprises. The
very term 'construction of a new society', born originally out of the
mistrust of the Bolsheviks for the natural processes of social development, acquired a totally concrete, material, technological meaning.

If the bourgeois modernization of Russia had ended in failure, the
bureaucratic project, which involved concentrating huge resources and
all the available social capital in the hands of the state, made it possible
to speed up rates of development several times over. This was done
without counting the cost which society was forced to pay for these
policies.

The new structures of government were aimed at maximizing the
speed and effectiveness with which these tasks could be fulfilled; for the
first time in human history, the structure of society became a direct
extension of the structure of administration. The ruling class merged
with the state to such a degree that it could no longer be termed a class
in the full sense. Civil society no longer existed; any human activity
which slipped out of the sphere of state administration was simply

crushed. The approach which had triumphed was consummately simple: whatever cannot be controlled should not exist.[2]

Everything served the principle of the simplification of control: all writers were grouped in a single union, as were all architects, artists and cinematographers. Peasants throughout the country were stripped of their own property and forced into collective farms, and small enterprises as far as possible were replaced by large ones, since this lightened the tasks of centralized control.

It is clear that for the bureaucracy the most natural methods were administrative ones. The experience of the New Economic Policy had shown that reliance on the market yielded only short-term results, helping to increase the quantity of goods in the shops and to strengthen people's faith in the regime, but not fulfilling the tasks of modernization. Capital investment remained weak, industry was still technically backward, and growth rates were inadequate and unstable. Administrative methods, on the other hand, allowed the new leaders quickly to concentrate resources around the main lines of advance – in the words of Stalin, finding the 'decisive link'. The country's rulers bothered little about the price of these successes.

A great deal is written nowadays about the inefficiency of Stalinist methods, about the great losses and the human sacrifices, since even if one ignores the moral implications, the death of millions of people hardly strengthened the country's economic potential. The main lesson which the regime learned from the defeat of Tsarist Russia was that even successful industrial development would not allow the country to stand on an equal footing with the West if the necessary rate of industrialization was not ensured, unless the necessary critical mass, allowing competition on an equal basis, was accumulated. From this point of view the regime was efficient. It did not ensure the production of quality goods, or increases in the standard of living, or high profitability in the enterprise. But it did guarantee dizzying rates of growth.

In essence, wrote the well-known Soviet sociologists L. Gordon and E. V. Klopov, this epoch gave birth to an astonishing 'mixture of progress, of the overcoming of backwardness, of outpourings of popular energy and enthusiasm, with phenomena of decay, stagnation, mass terror, and the collapse of the normal bases of social life'. A society arose in which 'labour was subordinated to a single discipline maintained by the state', and in which the state in turn guaranteed its citizens

a certain degree of social security – the absence of unemployment, the possibility of working and the obligation to do so, receiving a more or less

equal minimum of necessary socio-cultural benefits and obtaining other
goods in accordance with the results of their labour, the services they
rendered to society, and their social position.[3]

This system had nothing in common with the 'realm of liberty' of which
the founders of socialism had written. But millions of people,
exhausted by wars, stupefied by propaganda and inured to a daily
struggle for physical survival, accepted it as the highest expression of
social justice.

The whole society came to be divided into the controllers and the
controlled. From that point, naturally, the ordinary citizen existed only
as an object of control. How can one talk about human rights in such
circumstances?

The centralized apparatus of control was counterposed to the mass
of toilers who had been stripped of their rights. But the system was not
maintained only by terror and repression. After the traditional forms of
self-organization and the bonds between people had been liquidated,
the masses of the population, now essentially stripped of their class
identity, came to need the centralized state, without which they could
no longer fend for themselves. Between the individual and the state
there was no longer any intermediary; all the organizations fulfilling
this role – trade unions, voluntary associations, etc. – had themselves
become part of the state. The regime organized production, ensured the
instruction of children in the schools, guaranteed free health care,
provided work and organized recreation.

If this state with all its prisons, planning departments, repressive
apparatus and schools teaching not only literacy but also love for the
leaders had suddenly disappeared, society would have been doomed to
perish. People no longer possessed the habits of self-organization. They
knew nothing about one another. The viability of society, the stability
of production and consumption were guaranteed (though on the most
meagre level) by the very stability of the state system.

The comprehensive destruction of the class identity of the masses
began as early as the Stolypin reforms, which did not succeed in
creating a Russian farmer class, but which undermined the traditional
village community. The destruction of social bonds continued during
the First World War, the revolution and the Civil War. Millions of
people were plucked off their comfortable perches, cut off from their
relatives and accustomed surroundings. Workers migrated *en masse* to
the countryside, while peasants flooded the towns. In the years of the
New Economic Policy, when the peasants were permitted to work their
own land and a slow growth of industry began in the cities, a few signs

of social stabilization began to appear. But the violent collectivization of the countryside, accompanied by forced industrialization and terror, once again destroyed the insubstantial social fabric. Again millions of people moved from the countryside to the towns, in a matter of days transforming themselves from tillers of the soil to unskilled urban workers. The narrow stratum of hereditary proletarians was swept away by the wave of Stalinist industrialization.[4] The Second World War and the new waves of repression completed the deed. Society in the old sense of the word had simply ceased to exist. There was only the 'socio-political system'. Outside the structures of the state, social being and economic development had been made impossible.

This declassed society, robbed of stable social bonds, of tradition and culture, found control from outside indispensable. From then on the all-powerful bureaucracy not only guaranteed modernization, but also ensured the survival and reproduction of the population. This was why the system maintained its stability even after the mass terror came to an end in the 1950s.

The bureaucracy itself changed dramatically. It did not become a ruling class in the traditional Western sense of the term; classes only exist where there are social structures distinct from the structure of the state. But this was no longer the old state bureaucracy which had existed in Russia for centuries.

In European societies the bureaucracy usually executes the will of the ruling class. Naturally, the bureaucrats who administer the state also have their own personal interests. Very often the results of bureaucratic control turn out to be strikingly different from what is expected. But at the same time the apparatus does not advance its own goals and priorities. It merely interprets the will of the rulers after its own fashion as it implements their decisions.

Under the Soviet totalitarian system, by contrast, the apparatus both made the decisions and interpreted them. Without ceasing to be above all the executive apparatus of the regime, the bureaucracy no longer implemented the will of a ruling class, but took the place of the absent ruling class. In the strict sense it was no longer a bureaucracy on the old pattern, but a 'statocracy', a class-state or class-apparatus without property or stability. Mikhail Voslensky once ironically described the Soviet bureaucracy as a 'declassed class'. As has already been explained, in Stalinist society all classes in the strict sense were declassed, and in this respect the ruling elite was not so different from other social strata. But it had several important advantages: it was organized, and it had fused with the state power.

The ruling classes of 'normal' capitalist society have never been bound up with the state to such a degree. This has allowed them to ride out political crises with relative ease, changing governments and even, in some cases, the system of government. But for the statocracy any political crisis carried the threat of social catastrophe. The conservatism of the ruling circles was thus entirely natural.

The contradictory position of the ruling elite constantly gave rise to grotesque situations and often to breathtaking irresponsibility which ultimately harmed the interests of the bureaucracy itself. However, these weaknesses appeared in their full extent only later, when the system was disintegrating. In the initial periods the effectiveness of work within the apparatus was guaranteed with the help of terror, which touched the elite almost to the same extent as it affected those lower down, and by a sort of 'natural selection' in which the losers were physically liquidated.

Externally the system of control resembled a monolithic pyramid, beneath the foundations of which was a mass of workers, declassed and stripped of their rights. But closer scrutiny revealed that the 'monolith' was never entirely homogeneous. Within the 'great' pyramid of power were thousands of small and minute pyramids of control, each of them replicating the structure of the power system as a whole.

At the very pinnacle was located the 'great leader and teacher', Comrade Stalin, whose power was absolute. But every leading party boss within his province, every minister in his department, and every factory director within the confines of the plant was a little Stalin, holding sway over the life and death of his subjects. It is well known that Stalin's labour code, under which a worker could be jailed for turning up on the job twenty minutes late, gave factory directors complete control over the fate of their subordinates. Directors could hand people over to the NKVD for the slightest infraction, or could cover up gross breaches of discipline. The same principle applied in questions of production. The bosses' despotic power on the job guaranteed them considerable independence. The centre set the tasks and chose the people, whose lives then depended on the success of the undertaking. No one yet dreamed of planning every trifle from the centre. In the system as it then was, this was simply not required. All that was essential was to concentrate resources on the main lines of advance, to ensure the construction of the maximum possible number of heavy industrial enterprises in the shortest possible time, and to place control of these factories in the hands of 'loyal sons of the party'. There was no time to think of anything else. The system was primitive, but effective. Its primitiveness and simplicity were the reason for its success.

Industrial society was, in the main, established; the war was won; Russia, under the name of the Soviet Union, was transformed into a superpower. Economic growth continued, despite mounting difficulties.

But all this could not continue indefinitely.

The First Perestroika: the 1950s

The success of industrialization meant that society was qualitatively altered. Consequently, different methods of control were required. Already in the 1950s, when heavy industries had been established which were modern for those times, and when the economy had basically recovered from the destruction wrought by the Second World War, new problems began to arise. The Cold War and rivalry with the United States, the development of new military technologies, and the need for integration with the economies of Eastern Europe which had fallen into the Soviet sphere of influence, all served to confront the regime with the need for serious restructuring. The increased complexity of these tasks meant that it was already impossible to solve them by the original primitive methods. The unpaid labour of prisoners in the camps and forced labour in the cities had ceased to be effective. A new type of worker, able to master complex technology, was required.

Many scientists performed outstanding work in the *sharashki*, laboratory-prisons where scientific discoveries were made under the supervision of guards looking on through the bars. But it was impossible to organize mass production using such methods. Even in prison, geniuses might continue toiling for love of their work but ordinary skilled workers or engineers needed normal working conditions that allowed them to renew their capacity for labour, to gain access to necessary information in the normal fashion, and to undergo retraining. In short, the very minimum requirement was for free hired workers, who had to be provided with a standard of living and level of consumption which, if not equal to those in the West, were at least comparable. At least to a certain degree, it was necessary to guarantee workers their independence and rights, and for this it was essential to restrict the arbitrary power of the bosses in the workplaces, establishing definite general norms of conduct throughout the whole country.

The policy of 'thaw', introduced by Nikita Khrushchev after Stalin's death, was an attempt to carry out this task. The camps were dismantled. Powerful scientific research institutes were established on the basis of the *sharashki*, often headed by former inmates. A start was made

with modernizing the armed forces and renewing industrial technology. Right up until the end of the 1980s it was equipment installed
during the 1960s that formed the productive base in most enterprises.

Terror was replaced by gentler means of control, with the 'material
self-interest' of the worker coming to play an important role. The
consumer market began to develop rapidly. Despite the huge lag
behind the West in terms of living standards, the Soviet Union in the
1960s began to be transformed into a consumer society. This involved
not only substantial changes in the culture and psychology of the
workers, but also the formation of a new economic structure, capable
of producing not only tanks and tractors, but also goods meant for
people. From then on the population and the leadership itself formed
their opinions of the new system not only on the basis of its ability to
ensure the country's national independence, defensive might and 'great
power' status, or of its ability to provide the social equality promised by
the revolution, but also on the basis of its success in ensuring continual
increases in consumption.

The first social conflicts had already broken out by the beginning of
the 1960s, when a 'growth of popular well-being' had been promised
and the terror had come to an end, but the Stalinist economic system
was still unable to provide people with real improvements in their lives.
An acute crisis arose at the end of the 1950s and the beginning of the
1960s. A wave of strikes and uprisings swept through provincial
industrial centres. The biggest clash occurred in 1962 in Novocherkassk, when military forces fired on thousands of workers demonstrating beneath red banners.

During the years that followed the situation began to stabilize as
'perestroika' went ahead in the economy. The increase in Soviet living
standards at the end of the 1960s was rapid enough to win the
admiration of Western experts. The improvement in the lives of the
people was accompanied by the mastering of new technologies and
even by the conquest of leading positions in some areas of world
science. The Soviet economy was growing significantly faster than the
economies of the leading Western countries. Everything seemed to be
going wonderfully.

The pledge of 'steady increases in living standards' became the most
important element of the official ideology. The programme the CPSU
adopted under Khrushchev not only stated that communism would be
constructed by 1980, but also presented a picture of communism as a
society of consumer abundance. As now depicted by the official Soviet
ideologues, the ideal society was one of maximum consumption. It is
not surprising that a generation later many people in our country,

raised entirely in the spirit of Communist propaganda, not only see this ideal society in the West, but conclude in all seriousness that 'real socialism' has already been built in the United States or Canada.

If in Stalin's time the system was oriented towards economic growth at any price, from the 1960s the people were promised that economic growth would be accompanied by a rise in the standard of living. Just as in the West, the growth of consumption itself provided an important stimulus to economic growth. So long as the system retained its initial dynamism, this ideological model 'worked'. The 'consumer' model turned out to be even more stable than the Stalinist one, since social peace and the subservience of the masses could now be guaranteed without large-scale terror. But as the centralized economy lost its original capacity for effectively concentrating resources along the 'basic lines of advance', the situation deteriorated. The growth of living standards first slowed, then stopped altogether.

The worse the situation in the economy became, the more the ideology of consumerism turned against the system, which was incapable of fulfilling its own promises.

This, however, was to happen much later. In the 1950s the economy was 'normalized'. Along with Stalin's personal despotism in political life, the tyranny of the factory directors was consigned to the past. The process of 'normalizing' the system of rule had begun in essence even before Stalin died. The network of ministries and departments was streamlined and expanded, and new rules were adopted limiting the arbitrary powers (but also the freedoms) of the workplace bosses. The single system of power gradually branched out into several bureaucratic systems. Each department drew up its own 'nomenclature of official positions'. Transfers from one department to another, which had been typical for Stalin's 'nominees for promotion', became a rarity; the industrial bureaucracy became separated from the party apparatus, agricultural officialdom from that of the state, and so on.

The bureaucracy itself underwent changes. The struggles within the pyramid of power were continuous, but in Stalin's time a sort of 'natural selection' took place in the bureaucratic milieu. The struggle between groups and departments culminated in the physical annihilation of the losers. The people who survived in this system may have been thugs and criminals, but they were not passive nonentities.

Khrushchev's reforms meant the end of 'natural selection' in the ranks of the bureaucracy, which led to an abrupt decline in the effectiveness of the bureaucracy's actions. Khrushchev tried to preserve the dynamism of the apparatus by means of constant organizational shake-ups, but this contradicted the natural logic of the process of bureaucratic stabilization which he himself had begun. The period of 'thaw' was replaced by the epoch of 'stability'. In place of Khrushchev came Brezhnev.

It was quite clear that the system of government was becoming ever more complex and bureaucratized. The taking of any decision required the agreement of an ever greater number of people, while conflicts of interest began to arise between different bureaucracies. The party apparatus remained the core of the system, acquiring important new functions. It was not only required to rule the country, but also to co-ordinate the activity of the various bureaucracies, to act as arbitrator in conflicts, and to make the final decision in disputed cases. This in turn gave rise to new contradictions between the party apparatus and the 'economic managers'. On the one hand, the party elite meddled con-stantly in the affairs of the productive-sector bureaucracy, often defending non-economic interests, while, on the other hand, the elite ensured that the system retained a certain balance.

To the extent that the apparatus of economic management developed its own internal system of authority, the enterprise directors found themselves under dual control. In order for the central ministries and departments to manage the lower echelons effectively, they needed to obtain information on their activities and to assign them plan tasks through a system of 'indices' which made it possible to collect and evaluate information. The more complex and developed production became, the more indices were required. The more indices there were, the easier it became for enterprise directors and the ministries them-selves to manipulate them. The party authorities at the local level were much less interested in formal indicators, and much more interested in solving social problems and in making sure their decisions accorded with the ideological line of the party at a given stage.

From the point of view of the managers and their bureaucracy, the interference by the party was a hindrance so long as it failed to provide them with scarce supplies of raw materials, equipment and building materials. On the other hand, the meddling of the party apparatus allowed many industrial managers to manoeuvre between two forces: the local party authorities and the central ministries. The party appara-tus also provided a means of establishing horizontal links, direct informal contacts between the enterprises of different branches. Para-doxically, it was precisely the interference of the party organs which to a significant degree made up for the absence of a market structure.

The attempt in the period from 1965 to 1969 to streamline this system through decentralization and through broadening the rights of the managerial bureaucracy at the enterprise level ended in failure because the central departments and party bosses were unwilling to yield their authority. Nevertheless, something had to be changed. Amid constantly growing economic difficulties, an alternative was found in the form of bureaucratic decentralization. The centre was choking on information which it could not process in the required manner, but meanwhile it remained unwilling to yield its powers to people 'further down', especially since attempts at reform disturbed the equilibrium of the system, which despite its constantly increasing difficulties still worked after a fashion. The only alternative was to establish parallel centres.[5]

Ministries began to proliferate at an unbelievable rate. If this increased the degree of control within the branches, since each central department was now concerned with a smaller number of enterprises, the work of planning development and of reconciling conflicting interests became still more difficult, since a pluralism of bureaucratic interests had arisen. If the structure of power in the 1930s had called to mind a pyramid with the leader at its summit, by the 1970s this had become a complex structure with many summits, entangled in a spider's web of party organs.

Collapse

The system gradually became more benign. The totalitarian regime little by little turned into an authoritarian one, which no longer interfered in the private lives of its citizens and did not resort to large-scale terror – most of the structures indispensable for the everyday exercise of terror had already been dismantled in the course of the 1950s. To take any kind of decision was becoming more and more complex, but the methods of rule had, after their fashion, become more democratic, since neither the General Secretary nor the bosses further down could any longer ignore the opinions of their colleagues. Still, the might of the party and the dependence of workers on the state remained. It was still too early in the 1970s to speak of a real overthrow of totalitarianism.

In general, the mass of workers remained atomized. The migration of millions of people into the cities, which continued during the 1960s, made it difficult to form a hereditary working class, although by comparison with the epoch of Stalinist terror and war social bonds became stronger, and people now depended much less on the state.

The formation of new middle levels of society proceeded most rapidly of all. As the economy grew more complex it gave birth to a whole level of privileged scientific workers and managers. The new cultural requirements of the population called into being a whole industry of culture, including the rise of television and of a more sophisticated press. A new cultural elite was formed. The continuing shortage of goods and services at a time when living standards, purchasing power and demand were all on the increase created the conditions for the emergence of a developed and flourishing commercial mafia, which gradually penetrated into the most diverse areas of social life.

For all their heterogeneity, the middle levels were united by a similar pattern of life, with roughly the same educational standards and, finally, a uniform model of consumption. In conditions in which the culture and ideology of a new consumer society were being formed, this was very important.

At the same time, the middle levels were united by their contradictory relations with the authorities. Within the system almost all of these groups enjoyed privileges and rights which sharply elevated them above the mass of mere mortals. In some cases these rights were bestowed from on high, as with the intellectual elite who enjoyed all kinds of privileges, beginning with the right to additional living space in the midst of a housing shortage and ending with journeys abroad. Alternatively, the system of privileges was formed in a 'natural' manner, as occurred with managers, or the privileges were seized illegally on people's own initiative, as with the commercial mafia. In any case the system opened up far greater possibilities for the members of the middle levels than for 'ordinary' citizens. At the same time, the middle levels were completely alienated from real power. The inevitable interference in their affairs by the party apparatus provoked interminable conflicts. Finally, the middle strata possessed a much higher level of education and competence than the party functionaries who ruled over them; they were least of all in need of tutelage from the party apparatus. The middle levels were closer to the regime than anyone . . . and felt its pressure most strongly.

They felt the regime needed them, but denied them access to its ranks.

It was entirely natural that although the middle levels were not the most oppressed elements of society, it was here that aspirations for radical change began to arise most rapidly. It was here that an opposition began to form, and it was precisely in this milieu that ideas on a new social order began to take shape. Both the dissidents and the reformers emerged from the middle levels.

When the masses, driven to despair by poverty, powerlessness and unfulfilled promises, rose in revolt in Novocherkassk, they turned to the revolutionary traditions of 1917. The question of a reversion to capitalism was not even raised, just as an alternative socialist model was not advanced either. The people were simply demanding that the system fulfil its own promises of a life that accorded with the official slogans ('everything for the benefit of the worker', 'the only privileged class – children!' and so on). The same picture appears in the workers' uprisings in East Berlin in 1953 and in Poland in 1956 and 1970. But when the middle levels entered the fray, the demands were always for changing the rules of the game, for changing the structures of government and for sharing power. In this sense the opposition that came from the middle levels, for all its limitations, was uniquely 'constructive'; it was entirely natural that reformist ideas were far more influential than dissident ones, although the dissidents attracted more attention.

Because the middle levels were the only sector of society that had its own voice, and since they represented its only organized grouping, they began to speak in the name of the whole of society. In this situation the illusion that their own interests coincided completely with those of the country as a whole came to seem completely natural and just both to the reformers and to adherents of the dissident movement.

Meanwhile, the bureaucratization of the economy came to exceed any reasonable bounds, and the efficiency of production steadily declined. Growth rates fell persistently from 1959 on. If this did not attract attention in the first years, by the end of the 1970s the situation had changed. By this time it had become impossible not only to wage a struggle against the United States for world hegemony, but also to fulfil the promises made to the Soviet Union's own people. Social stability, which had been purchased at the cost of transition to a consumer economy, was undermined. Even the ruling circles began to recognize that reforms were indispensable.

If the task of totalitarianism had consisted in maximizing the degree of control over every social process on the basis of a single integrated system of rule, then it was natural that the loosening of controls within the system and the loss of its integral character would lead to a serious political and economic crisis. As the system of total control became less and less effective and began to collapse, Soviet and East European society was to pass through a whole series of such crises.

The difficulties increased throughout the 1960s and 1970s. By the beginning of the 1980s the Soviet state, in the apt comparison of Bulat Okudzhava, had come to recall 'the Roman Empire in the era of its collapse'. The crisis of control demoralized the ruling circles, and undermined their faith in the viability of the system even more than the slowing growth rates of the economy and the growing dissatisfaction of the people. To take any decision was becoming ever more difficult, the bureaucratic labyrinths were becoming more and more involved, to the point where even experienced professional functionaries found themselves at a loss.

If the apparatus was complaining about a 'lowering of the effectiveness of administration', the working population and the lower managerial levels were being made to pay the price for the system's collapse. By the end of the 1970s the crisis of administration had given birth to a 'crisis of supply'. Shortages became an everyday problem not only for the ordinary consumer, but also for factory directors. The centralized system of distribution of resources suffered ever worse breakdowns, planned deliveries were not made, and it was impossible to find out where goods had finished up. The paradoxical reaction of the administrative apparatus to the collapse of the supply system was to form a sort of 'grey market' – direct links were established between enterprises, which did not so much buy products from one another as exchange goods in short supply. Everyone who succeeded in gaining access to 'deficit' goods, whether they were a housewife or the director of an automobile plant, began to build up their stocks. The ordinary Soviet apartment became more and more like a warehouse. The satirist Zhvanetsky noted that at home he lived 'as if in a submarine'; he could hold out on his own for a month.

The development of barter and direct links, together with the accumulation of 'hidden reserves', rendered the work of the central supply system still more difficult and further reduced the effectiveness of administration. Simultaneously, the country was hit by a crisis of investment. With the central organs lacking precise information on what was going on, and resources being distributed spontaneously through the 'grey' and 'black' markets, it was impossible to complete state investment projects on time. For the departments, meanwhile, the construction of new enterprises became the most reliable means of obtaining additional resources from the centralized funds. Construction projects were begun, but not finished. Capital investments did not bring returns.

This in turn became one of the most important sources of inflation. The constantly growing volume of uncompleted construction work became the breach through which billions of rubles not backed by actual goods flowed into the economy. The money invested in the construction of new enterprises not only failed to produce profits, but also brought about new shortages, demanded new spending, went to purchase labour power which did not create any final product that could be sold on the market. The financial crisis led to the accumulation by enterprises and the population of savings worth many billions, of which only a part was held in savings accounts and in the banks. The rest remained in the hands of the population, filled various 'black accounts' or circulated on the black market.

As a result of the collapse of the official mechanisms of control a sort of shadow system of administration began to form spontaneously, and to merge directly with the criminal underworld.

As a general rule, corruption is the natural outgrowth of an inefficient bureaucracy. In any society the level of corruption is in inverse proportion to the effectiveness of administration. But in Soviet society the mafia not only grew rich on the failures of the system, but in fact began to transform itself into a shadow regime, much more efficient and stable than the officially proclaimed one.

By the beginning of the 1980s the disintegration of the system was already obvious. Using the last of its strength, the Brezhnev leadership tried to give the impression that nothing was happening in the country, but the bureaucracy itself, every day running up against the crisis of administration, demanded changes. The trouble was that this time the regime had no reserves left. The system could no longer be reconstructed; its disintegration had proceeded too far. The collapse of the Communist state in Poland and the failure of the reforms in Hungary showed that the collapse of the structure had acquired a universal character, that it was not a specifically Soviet phenomenon. In essence, the entire East European bloc was in crisis by the 1980s.

The Heirs of Totalitarianism

The attempts to reform the mechanisms of power not only failed to give the expected results but, on the contrary, exacerbated the crisis. The ailing administrative machine could not guarantee the effective implementation of reforms even where successes might in theory have been registered. Meanwhile, the efforts of the ruling circles to introduce new economic mechanisms gradually, strengthening the role of market relations and establishing new structures that would be more representative and democratic, served to destroy the remains of the old mechanism rather than to construct a new one. (Remember the old joke about how, as an experiment, it was decided to switch half of the transport system to driving on the left.)

By the end of the 1980s it was clear to everyone that the system had reached an impasse. If Gorbachev and those around him in the first years after their rise to power could console themselves with illusions about a 'reconstruction' ('perestroika') of society, by 1988–89 the situation had finally run out of control. The bureaucratic apparatus itself had finally lost its cohesion, and had collapsed into warring rival groups. One ministry would go on the offensive against other ministries, one republic against another, and all joined in attacking the central government and party apparatus which were trying to bring some kind of order to this chaos.

During the initial stages the party apparatus still maintained a certain stability, but in conditions of general collapse it could not hold out for long. The struggle of factions and groups intensified, the more so because the party elite was never completely homogeneous. In Eastern Europe the old order fell apart even more rapidly, though in each country the process had its own distinctive features.

By 1990 the only country in Eastern Europe where a traditional 'Communist' regime remained intact was Albania. Elsewhere the Communist parties' monopoly on power had been abolished, and the centralized administration of the economy liquidated. Free elections were held even in Mongolia, and everywhere policies of privatizing the state sector began to be implemented. At first glance it might have seemed that Russia and Eastern Europe were undergoing a transition from 'communist totalitarianism' to Western-style capitalist democracy. But in reality what was occurring was something quite different.

One important condition for a transition to capitalism was absent: in none of these countries was there a developed bourgeoisie. And for the establishment of Western-style democracy a small requirement was missing: developed structures of civil society.

If in Eastern Europe during the early stages people had been able to comfort themselves with the illusion that as 'historical parts of Europe' their countries by some miracle would in a few months establish all the indispensable social and historical conditions for democratic capitalism, in Russia the situation was qualitatively worse. The incongruence of the Western and Eastern models of society was obvious. It was simply impossible to understand the processes unfolding in the East by means of analogies with the West. Society to a significant degree remained declassed; people were not conscious of their interests, and the normal social bonds were missing. There were no classes. The mass movement was inevitably transformed into the actions of a mob. People were accustomed to relying on the state for help, and to protesting against the injustices of the state, but they had no experience of life in a society where the state was powerless, and citizens had to solve their problems independently. In essence, the only forces in the East with a degree of social organization remained the bureaucracy and the middle levels.

The old nomenklatura, which through its rule had led the countries into crisis, remained the sole social group capable of controlling the situation. The nomenklatura could no longer rule in the old fashion, but no one could take its place at the helm of the state administration. Political slogans could be changed, and new ideological labels could be pasted on to the state, but the fact remained: looming up ahead was a crisis and no alternatives. There was no new class able to seize power from the old oligarchy and to give shape to a new model of society. Only the oligarchy itself, or some part of it, could do this.

None of the political observers, it appears, has paid any attention to one particularly striking fact. During 1989 and 1990 a powerful opposition movement arose swiftly in the USSR. It won representation in the Supreme Soviet, led crowds of many thousands through the streets, and gained control of Moscow and Leningrad. But with the exception of Andrei Sakharov, who played a mainly symbolic role, hardly any of the old dissidents assumed important posts in this new opposition. Many of them emigrated, while others were unwilling to play according to the rules laid down by Gorbachev. All of the key roles in the present-day opposition have been filled by people from the old apparatus. Boris Yeltsin, Yuri Afanasyev, Nikolai Travkin, Ivan Silayev who became Prime Minister of Russia after the opposition victory in the republican elections, and Moscow Mayor Gavriil Popov all occupied important posts in the old system. And most remarkably, it was precisely their positions in the system which allowed them to become political leaders.

Hardly anyone would have been interested in Yeltsin had he not, at the beginning of this process, been a candidate member of the Politburo of the CPSU. If Yuri Afanasyev had not been rector of a historico-archival institute, and earlier still one of the leaders of the Communist Youth League, his name would hardly be known even among historians. If these people had not been participants in exercising power it is even more unlikely that they would have been able to publish their views in the official press, control of which was still monopolized by the state until the middle of 1990.

The nomenklatura could no longer rule in the old fashion, but it quickly learned to rule according to the new. In order to retain and strengthen their positions in the new circumstances, the ruling circles had themselves to form a new model of power and a new structure of property.

When a wave of 'bloodless revolutions' rolled through Eastern Europe, and when in 1990 the supreme authorities in the USSR allowed the holding of elections which gave majorities in republican soviets to the opposition, almost no one asked the question: why did the ruling circles surrender political power so easily? One cannot explain this rapid and general capitulation simply by the fact that the East European leaders were 'demoralized' or had lost the support of Moscow. In the past, 'Communist' regimes had readily slaughtered thousands of people, crushing the slightest protest movement. How a Stalinist government behaved when it really had its back to the wall we saw in the case of Romania, where the dictatorship of Nicolae Ceausescu only fell after two weeks of bloodshed. But even in Romania the overthrow of the regime took the form of a palace coup, in which a significant part of the old apparatus not only failed to oppose the revolution, but actively participated in it, ensuring that the armed forces and the police would pass over to the side of the people in the first hours of the uprising. What was under threat was above all the personal power of the dictator and his entourage. For those sections of the nomenklatura which were not personally linked to the Ceausescu family, the changes even turned out to be advantageous.

It is easy to understand that in the new circumstances the ruling circles cannot sustain their power using the old methods. The collapse of the single monolithic apparatus of government generates new alliances. The old rulers turn to collaborating with the middle levels, naturally sharing power with them, while the dealers of the 'shadow economy' are given the chance to 'go legal' and to swell the ranks of an 'official', legitimate ruling class. By the end of 1990 the Communist Party of the Soviet Union was already the largest entrepreneur in the country, taking part in property speculation, founding commercial banks, hard-currency hotels and so on. The pages of Soviet newspapers were full of reports of business activity by the party apparatus. Most of this new party business was concentrated in the sphere of services, property speculation and financial dealings.[6] The property of the party organs was little by little turning into the property of the party apparatchiks.

It was also considered opportune to open the door to foreign capital, and here as well the 'new' bourgeois relations were intertwined with the old bureaucratic system. The Soviet press lamented:

Former economic managers, party officials, activists in the Communist Youth League and trade union functionaries, sensing the tenuousness of their positions in the nomenklatura and the advantages of international collaboration, have begun to exploit their contacts and have been among the first to reach agreement with Western businessmen on establishing joint ventures.[7]

Even if foreign capitalists had wanted to find other partners in Eastern Europe and Russia, they could not have done so. In the former Eastern bloc property only exists where there is power. In conditions of crisis the ruling elite is ready to share both power and property, but not to surrender them. And most importantly, there is no one to surrender them to.

In the final analysis, despite all the changes which have occurred in society, a new elite is nonetheless forming on the basis of the old bureaucracy.

Maintaining a monopoly of state property had advantages for the bureaucracy so long as it remained united and was capable of exercising full control over all the structures of the state. But in conditions in which the unified apparatus of power has fallen apart, the bureaucrats have found it more advantageous simply to divide up the property among themselves.

In this manner, the bureaucratic pluralism which came into being in the 1970s prepared the way for the rise of capitalist private property. But this does not by any means signify the rise of an entrepreneurial bourgeoisie. Quite the contrary. As before, property and power remain indissolubly linked. But whereas in the past the possession of power meant that one could control property only through illegitimate means, today power can be turned 'legally' into property ownership.

Notes

1. Trotsky, *Chto takoe SSSR i kuda on idyot?* ('The Revolution Betrayed'), Paris 1988, p. 127.
2. In this, moreover, there is a substantial difference between the totalitarianism of the twentieth century and traditional Asiatic despotism. Parallels between the Soviet regime of the Stalin period and the 'Asiatic mode of production' have been drawn repeatedly both by Marxist and non-Marxist scholars. In this and other cases property becomes concentrated in the hands of a despotic state, there is a connection between power and ideology (in the ancient Asiatic variant, the special role of the state religion and of the priestly caste), and in both cases an effort is made to exercise central control over economic processes. But in the 'Asiatic' variant what is involved is constant work by the state to ensure simple reproduction (the maintenance of irrigation systems, the setting of annual norms for the delivery of grain to the village communes and so forth), while in our case the task posed is one of forced economic growth and the replacement of old pre-industrial technologies by new industrial ones. The character of the state is thus completely different. Within the framework of the 'Asiatic' system the state exercised unlimited power, but it had no pretensions to total control over society. Moreover, the basic processes occurring at the base were self-

regulating. The communities were ruled by customary law, and in political terms they enjoyed considerable autonomy. By contrast, the totalitarianism of the twentieth century was constructed according to the principle of total, all-encompassing control. On 'Asiatic despotism' and totalitarianism, see B. Kagarlitsky, *Dialektika nadezhdy* ('The Dialectics of Hope'), Paris 1989.

3. L. A. Gordon and E. B. Klopov, *Chto eto bylo?* ('What Was That?'), Moscow 1989, p. 149.

4. For a more detailed treatment, see L. A. Gordon and A. K. Nazimova, *Rabochiĭ klass SSSR: tendentsii i perspektivy sotsial 'no-ekonomicheskogo razvitiya* ('The Working Class of the USSR: Tendencies and Perspectives of Socio-Economic Development'), Moscow 1985.

5. For a detailed analysis of bureaucratic decentralization under Brezhnev, see B. Kagarlitsky, *The Dialectic of Change*, London 1989.

6. Detailed information on the business activities of the CPSU can be found in journals such as *Gorizont*, *Argumenty i Fakty* and *Kommersant*.

7. *Stolitsa*, 1990, no. 1, p. 37.

2

Intellectuals versus the
Intelligentsia: A Crisis of Culture?

As is well known, the first manifestation of perestroika was glasnost. While political transformations were still being discussed in the kitchen, and Gorbachev was holding forth on single-party democracy and proving that the concept of 'Stalinism' had been invented by enemies of the USSR in order to undermine our society, material which shortly before had been prohibited was beginning to appear in newspapers and literary journals. The publication of books written twenty years before provoked stormy arguments, and a congress of cinematographers turned into a major political event. However, this did not continue for long.

After a certain point journalists ceased to talk about the new 'frontiers of glasnost'. Out of inertia the literary process still proceeded from sensation to sensation, but more and more of the sensations were from the past, and interest in them gradually waned.

The most intense interest and the sharpest controversies were evoked by Anatoly Rybakov's novel *Children of the Arbat*, which for all its virtues was clearly not a great literary masterpiece. Vasily Grossman's *Life and Fate* was politically much more acute, and unquestionably more significant in artistic terms, but the impact on society of its publication was much less. In 1989 *Novy Mir* published Solzhenitsyn's *Gulag Archipelago*. Soon after its distribution the book disappeared from sight. I recall someone writing in one of the samizdat journals that if the *Archipelago* were to be published in an edition of millions, everything would be overturned. The book was duly published. But has anything been overturned, even in literature?

Of course, even in 1989 the works of some writers were still banned – for example, the works Trotsky wrote in exile, including his remarkable autobiography. Apparently these books were considered even more threatening than the *Gulag Archipelago*. But at the end of 1990 the first collection of Trotsky's works from the post-October period appeared in the bookstores, and publishers, sensing that there were profits to be made, began to discuss publishing the writings in exile of the 'last Bolshevik'. It is clear that in the new situation the publication of this book will not set off any shock waves either.

So what is going on? For the first year or two after the proclamation of glasnost the critics all demanded to know: where are the new names, where are the new works? The massive interest in literature, it transpired, was being aroused almost exclusively by the return to print of books released from censorship, and by the publication of memoirs seized from desk drawers. But after voicing their complaints the critics virtually ceased to discuss this topic. They had, it seems, grown used to the situation.

Of course, new books also appeared. But once again, most of them were concerned with the past. Anatoly Pristavkin's book *A Golden Cloud Stayed Overnight* is already a classic of the literature of the 1980s. But where are the books about the 1980s? One could cite Yuri Polyakov's *Apofegey* and a few similar short stories, but this is hardly enough to satisfy someone interested in serious prose.

So, is there a crisis in literature? And is that all? Listen to people from the theatre and the cinema, and you will find a similar picture. The congress of cinematographers which marked the beginning of glasnost quickly became legendary, but the heroes of the first years of perestroika came under criticism from colleagues who accused them of usurping power and of political egoism.

In my view, behind these outwardly visible crises lies another crisis, much more profound and serious – a crisis of the intelligentsia. It is not only the conditions for creative activity that have changed; stereotypes of behaviour, principles and key values have changed as well. Why was it that ten years ago some people went to prison for distributing the *Gulag Archipelago*, even if they did not agree with the author's ideas, while others cruelly persecuted them for this (as it turned out) not very threatening activity? Both the persecutors and their victims believed in the power of the word, that it was dangerous in and of itself. This traditional Russian and Eastern notion, alas, is vanishing before our eyes. The place of the cult of the word is being taken by the traditional principle of liberal Western culture, repressive tolerance: you can say whatever you like, but it will change little or nothing. The writer can no longer change the world. He or she merely provides goods for the book trade.

The truth is that it will be a long time before we can provide high-quality products even for this market. The stereotypes of Western culture 'work' within the framework of a liberal-democratic society. But where is our liberal democracy?

Prosperous Radicals

The traditional Russian concept of the intelligentsia differs substantially from that of 'the intellectuals' in the West. The Russian intelligentsia were mainly Westernizers, nourished on Western influences – first on Hegel and Schelling (incidentally, who now recalls the huge influence Schelling exerted on the slavophiles?), then on Mill and Marx.The intelligentsia seized on the most advanced and radical of Western culture. But they were still clearly unlike their Western colleagues. Intellectuals, according to the definition of Jean-Paul Sartre, are the 'technicians of practical knowledge'. Workers in the field of mental labour, they possess indispensable skills and information, and use them to earn their daily bread. The role of intellectual does not automatically presuppose any moral norms or principles of behaviour, just as it is not linked to any particular political orientation. The Russian concept of the intelligentsia, meanwhile, is quite different.

The traditional role of the intelligentsia is to speak out in the name of the people against the undemocratic state: the intelligentsia defends not its own interests, but those of the oppressed, viewing its activity as closely connected with the struggle for democracy. It is precisely these moral principles which used to bind the intelligentsia into a single whole. This unity was embodied in the 'thick journals', a literary form inconceivable in the West, which arose among us in the nineteenth century, and in each issue of which one could read prose, poetry and articles on economics and the natural sciences. Both the authors and readers understood that all this was directed towards a single goal.

A natural consequence of this ideology was that the intelligentsia was oriented towards socialism as the most consistent form of democratic movement. Even among supporters of the Constitutional Democrats socialist ideas enjoyed great popularity. When, following the 1905 revolution, a group of the most prominent thinkers of the time – N. Berdyayev, S. Bulgakov, P. Struve and others – turned abruptly to the right, publishing the collection Vekhi ('Landmarks'), they made a sharp critique not only of the revolution and of socialism, but also of the intelligentsia.

The new intelligentsia consciously or unconsciously viewed itself as the continuation of the pre-revolutionary one, and with a certain justification. A similar situation had arisen, and along with it similar basic ideas and values, including a belief in socialist ideas and some kind of aspiration to defend the interests of the masses. During the 1960s the journal *Novy Mir* was steeped in these sentiments. Representatives of the generation of the 1960s remain faithful to these ideas. But on the whole, the situation has changed radically.

A kind of mutation has taken place. This occurred as early as the 1970s, though the lack of glasnost meant that no one paid attention to it. The dissolution of the editorial board of *Novy Mir* and the political crackdown of the time did not affect the daily lives of the intelligentsia. The Brezhnev regime repressed only those who protested openly, only those who overstepped certain bounds. Otherwise, people continued to publish books, to speak at symposiums and to travel abroad. The regime did not even demand loyalty; it was enough, in the memorable phrase of L. M. Batkin, to make a 'ritual self-defilement', attending unpleasant gatherings, knowing when to keep one's mouth shut, voting for the single candidate and so on. The material position and social status of the intellectual elite improved substantially in this period. Instead of shared communal flats they had private co-operative apartments. Volga and Mercedes cars appeared, while tape recorders and even computers became a norm of consumption.

I have no wish to sound off against material well-being. It would be cynical and vulgar to reduce the debate to this level. But one must recognize that on the psychological level the decade-long combination of political pressure and material prosperity had unexpectedly destructive consequences for the spiritual world of our intelligentsia. It has been comic to watch certain moralists among our writers protesting against 'consumerism ' in our country where even the purchase of a piece of soap is becoming difficult. But the fact is that the moralists have been solving their own ethical problems.

The price of prosperity was conformism, and the psychological defence against conformism was cynicism. This was against a background of growing despair among the intelligentsia about a democratic future for the country and of a political future for their own social stratum. The generation of the 1960s tried to hold fast to their principles, but the people of the 1970s became a lost generation. For ten years new literary figures virtually ceased to appear. One can mention Gelman, Petrushevskaya, Makanin and a few others, but there can be no comparison with the literary 'explosion' of the 1960s.

In the middle of the 1980s, by which time an important part of the intelligentsia had lost all hope, the situation changed abruptly and decisively. Perestroika was proclaimed, and the intelligentsia suddenly regained its voice. But the sound of this voice was now completely different.

From Lenin to Reagan

On the ideological level the first two years of perestroika saw a *revanche* by the people of the 1960s. Representatives of this generation were unexpectedly thrust to the forefront, many of them acquiring real power. It seemed that 'liberal communism', which had inspired the intelligentsia of the Khrushchev era and had collapsed following the entry of Soviet forces into Czechoslovakia, had gained its second wind. People once again believed in the possibility of gradual reforms from above. They believed that a liberal market reform, viewed as a second edition of Lenin's New Economic Policy, might proceed under the direction of party leaders who recognized their historic responsibilities, and might gradually and smoothly bring us to democracy. Meanwhile the progressive intelligentsia would aid this process by giving advice and constructive criticism.

The arguments of the supporters of change were often extremely superficial, but a society striving to free itself from the quagmire of Brezhnevite 'stability' received them with enthusiasm. In essence, a new mythology was created, which in its initial period was closely linked to the old ideology. If Stalin, Khrushchev and Brezhnev had claimed to represent the 'heritage' of Lenin, then perestroika had now in turn to express the true essence of Leninism.

The authentic face of Leninism would now be associated with the New Economic Policy of the 1920s. Accordingly, NEP was described as a period of rapid economic growth, flourishing culture and political liberalism. Naturally, the authors of the numerous articles on NEP closed their eyes to the fact that it was precisely during the period of NEP that the single-party system was finally consolidated, that repression began against opposition socialist parties which until then had been semi-legal, that factions were outlawed within the Bolshevik party itself, and that increasing numbers of the intelligentsia began to emigrate. The authors of these articles also neglected to note that economic growth was achieved mainly through the simple restoration of pre-war levels of output, that investment was conspicuously weak, and that growth rates steadily declined from the mid-1920s. The authors were reluctant to discuss the fact that it was precisely under the new market conditions that the government had suffered a rapid bureaucratization which, the Bolsheviks themselves admitted, exceeded anything that had occurred during the Civil War. In short, they stubbornly refused to see the significance of NEP as a transitional period which allowed the bureaucracy to stabilize itself and to prepare the way for the final transition to Stalinist totalitarianism.

As part of the logic of this political and cultural *revanche*, the 'judgement of history' on the Stalinist past was moved to centre-stage. Blackened names were rehabilitated, and banned books returned to the bookstores. For a time our periodical press turned into a gigantic literary archive. But there was no way we could move forward with our faces turned to the past. It quickly became apparent that behind the general aspiration for change there were contradictory interests, and that the economic reform, involving a strange – but in current circumstances entirely logical – combination of traditionally bureaucratic, market and capitalist measures, brought real gains only to the most modern sectors of the apparatus, to the technocrats, to the provincial mercantile bourgeoisie (who for some reason where known as 'co-operators') and at times to the international corporations which were quickly grafting themselves on to the traditional bureaucratic nomen-klatura through a system of 'joint ventures'. During the struggles which surrounded the reforms most social strata quickly came to recognize where their interests lay. The masses discovered that the changes gave them nothing but the chance to express their dissatisfaction openly, and responded by going on strike.

Meanwhile, in place of the old intelligentsia's concern for the well-being of the masses something new was emerging: a cult of competence, a desire to defend one's own 'departmental' interests. There is nothing inherently bad in this. When I see the determination with which representatives of the creative arts in the Supreme Soviet defend their unions' right to tax privileges, I can only rejoice at the fact that these organizations have finally found a leadership capable of standing up for the interests of their members. But what a departure this represents from the traditional role of the intelligentsia, always prepared to sacrifice its interests for the good of the people. It was no accident that at a critical early stage in his literary career Dostoevsky found himself in prison, which was also where Chernyshevsky ended his career. Nor was it accidental that in Russia at the beginning of the twentieth century the intelligentsia and revolutionary sympathies were regarded as almost synonymous. Rejection of this history and this tradition amounts to rejection of the main element in the identity of the

Russian intelligentsia.

The 1960s-style liberals found themselves on the defensive. Taking over from them were the more consistent champions of neoliberal ideology, supporters of Mrs Thatcher and Ronald Reagan. We may like their views or we may not, but whatever the case, these views were much more logical than those of the liberal Communists. And indeed, if the slogans of the day are the 'free market' and the right of the 'advanced minority' to implement reform in its own interests, sacrificing the interests of the 'backward majority' (remember the motifs of the 1930s?); if on the pages of Novy Mir, once famous for its defence of the rights of the individual, we are reminded of the need to reconcile ourselves to the existence of tens of millions of unemployed; in short, if we are called upon to act in the same way as right-wingers in the West act and propagandize, then what is the point of talking about socialism? Why return to 'true Leninism', or to the experience of the 1920s? The consistent neoliberals saw in all these ideological references nothing more than a tribute to tradition and to political circumstances, a temporary cover which now, in conditions of glasnost, is no longer required.

Rejecting the dogmas of the past has become a sacred act. But is it not obvious that as well as rejecting the last vestiges of socialist ideology we are also saying farewell to humanism, to the traditional democratic mission of the intelligentsia, which always used to understand democratic values not just in terms of Western liberal institutions (for example, those in South Africa) but in terms of the interests of the majority? The history of Vekhi is repeating itself.

The breakdown of the stereotypes traditionally used for understanding the consciousness of the intelligentsia has been accompanied by the formation of a technocratic worldview. The new Russian intellectuals are also attracted to the West, but for them the West is no longer three thousand years of civilization, Voltaire, Modigliani or Marx, but technology and consumption. The yearning after this earthly paradise dictates policies oriented towards the copying of Western methods regardless of whether they accord with our social, cultural and economic conditions. A concern for culture is relegated to second place, if it continues to play any role at all. Literature, the theatre and the cinema must all, in line with the conceptions of an archaic, savage capitalism, simply become commodities. What else can one expect in our current circumstances? What we are seeing is not the formation of a new culture, but merely the destruction of the old.

Neoconformism

Glasnost revealed the striking spiritual poverty of that significant part of society which under the new conditions could think of nothing better than to reverse the black and white tones on the old ideological snapshots or to borrow propaganda clichés from the past. When it was explained that everything was permitted, the conformist stereotypes of behaviour did not collapse but merely acquired new content. In place of the expected pluralism, the heavyweight journals and weekly newspapers in many cases came to display a striking uniformity – at least compared with social thinking in the West. The compulsion to jump on the bandwagon, and if possible, to be 'in the forefront of progress', forced ideologues to compete in mouthing the general positions of liberalism. The results have often been quite comic. *Literaturnaya Gazeta* published a new critique of Berdyayev, who was always accused of failing to realize or understand something. This time he was charged with having failed to realize 'the truth of capitalism', and having failed to completely overcome Marxist influences on his work. The utterly confused readers, who at that time were still unable to peruse the works of Berdyayev for themselves (his writings were not published in the USSR until the end of 1990), could only raise their hands in bewilderment.

The news-stands are now packed with publications telling us of the evil deeds of the Bolsheviks who killed the last Russian tsar, and criticism of Trotsky and Trotskyism is reaching a scale not seen since Stalin's time. In issue after issue newspapers and journals write about the horrors of the Red Terror of 1918–21; it is now attracting more attention than the terror of the 1930s. This has been inspired not only by the evolution of the ideologues to whom the pages of our leading publications have been given over, but also by the logic of the new market; they have already written about Stalin and Stalinism, and new goods are needed.

The condemnation of the Red Terror is the natural result of open debate about the past. It is impossible to write truthfully about the revolution without telling the truth about its actions; one cannot remain silent about the rivers of innocent blood that were spilt. But the blood did not flow exclusively on one side, and this is the fundamental difference between the events of 1918–21 and those of the 1930s. V. G. Korolenko, L. Martov and other Russian ideologues who dared to speak out against the Red Terror during the years of the Civil War simultaneously described the crimes of the White Guards. They condemned the Red Terror not because it was 'Red', but because they opposed terror in general, just as they opposed all the political and social violence that was scourging Russia during those years. We hear nothing of the kind from our present-day liberal writers. They have no problems with White Terror. Not one of them has condemned the Red Terror from a general humanist standpoint. Their critique of Bolshevism is conducted exclusively from the positions of the White movement.[1]

Can it be true that the Moscow intelligentsia, many of whose members are the grandchildren and great-grandchildren of Bolshevik activists, who spent many years in the Communist Party and who punctiliously carried out the political rituals of the Brezhnev regime, have suddenly become (or always secretly were) convinced monarchists and admirers of the White generals? Hardly. It is more likely that this is simply an indication of the new fashions. In polite society these days it is simply not done to talk about the crimes of the Whites. On the other hand, it is perfectly acceptable to talk and write about the atrocities of the Reds. That's a saleable commodity. Serious literature and serious history, however, demand a principled rejection of the 'commercial approach'. The ability to resist fashion, to stand up to prevailing ideological trends and to the pressures of the market is no less important than a preparedness to stand up to the state. It was precisely this ability that distinguished the 'traditional' intelligentsia. Meanwhile, just at the moment when the repressions of the state have changed to repressive tolerance, most of our writers have shown a striking incapacity to make independent cultural and ideological choices. We swim with the current, and while enjoying the delights of glasnost, we are obviously losing our inner freedom.

What does this mean for art? In my view, the consequences are likely to be catastrophic.

Can one write propaganda poems in favour of 'commercial skills'? Or even 'the freedom to trade' and 'the free market'? Yes, but only bad poems. The praise of authoritarianism and industrialization in the poems of Mayakovsky outrages present-day critics, who see in this a degeneration of his talent. Many present-day writings glorifying the rights of the strong, waxing rapturous at the art of commerce and preaching a philistine 'common sense' as the supreme virtue, sound no less monstrous. But among these people there is no new Mayakovsky.

The mentality which underlies the new popular ideas is thoroughly traditional. A minority claims the right to use violence against the majority in the name of the well-being of that majority. The development of the economy and the construction of modern enterprises is seen as the sole criterion of progress. If the Bolsheviks saw the economy as one big factory, then according to the new liberals society and the economy should be run as one gigantic supermarket. In their symmetrical illusions and simplistic approach to reality the present-day preachers of simple solutions are like the early Stalinists of the 1920s. In both cases distorted conceptions of radicalism and progress lie at the bottom of everything. In both cases the acceptance of such logic even by a part of the intelligentsia testifies to its profound crisis.

In the West it has long been recognized that a writer can have right- or left-wing views, but that the political ideas of a left-wing writer usually find a direct reflection in his or her creative work, while among right-wingers this is not the case. A striking recent example is Mario Vargas Llosa, the political content of whose writing diminished as he was drawn into politics as a right-wing activist. The point is that the Western 'leftist intellectual' is more or less close to the traditional Russian intelligentsia. In destroying our traditions, we also cut one of the most important threads connecting us with the West.

Intellectuals have little in common with one another; there is nothing that links economic experts to specialists on literature. From the moment when the logic of the economic broadsides in the heavyweight journals begins increasingly to contradict the humanist principles which still find expression in the prose, there is less and less need for the two to be united in one volume. The only real reasons nowadays are savings in paper and convenience in postage. But the number of subscriptions is still diminishing.

From this point of view, the position expressed by I. Klyamkin and A. Migranyan in their joint interview with *Literaturnaya Gazeta* is thoroughly natural and logical. Paradoxically, this interview became the main cultural event of 1990, since it signalled the collapse of the last myths which the intelligentsia tried to foster about itself.

Klyamkin and Migranyan spoke of the need for dictatorship, arguing that without it the market economy would not work in our country. I would agree completely, with one reservation: it would probably not work under a dictatorship either. A real solution to the crisis demands a huge mobilization of resources and labour power around the basic priorities of development, and this, as the experience of the 1930s showed, could be achieved only through totalitarian planning, or through some form of democratic regulation which still remains to be established. But this is not the topic of the present discussion. The majority of critics attacked Klyamkin and Migranyan from the position of general values and the general good, whereas in reality the article in question was not about this at all, but was about private interests. In essence they were simply explaining to us in a popular way that certain social strata, including the intellectual elite, would find it more agreeable living under a liberal-authoritarian market regime than in conditions of democracy or in the situation which is developing today.

Not everyone considered it necessary to take their distance from Klyamkin and Migranyan, even verbally. The closer the country came to implementing the liberal project, the greater the number of its supporters who began talking about the 'firm hand'. In the autumn of 1990 the historian A. Kiva declared in *Izvestiya* that 'democracy, that is the power of the people, may turn into the power of the mob', and that in an epoch of crisis 'the guarantee of success in every country of the world has been authoritarian power'.[2] One can only marvel at the historical erudition of an author who can assess the experience of every country in the world. But when the issue is one of dictatorship, theoretical disputes become meaningless. The central and most substantial argument of the supporters of coercive power always turns out to be power itself – control of a sufficient quantity of tanks and machine-guns, and above all, of people in the tanks who will not hesitate to fire on an unarmed crowd.

It is not hard to see the resemblance with the events surrounding the journal *Vekhi*. Of course, I am not about to place Klyamkin and Migranyan on the same level as such thinkers as Berdyayev or Bulgakov, but the similarity of their conclusions is obvious. The most striking thing, however, is the fact that despite the critical statements from many writers which appeared in *Literaturnaya Gazeta*, the article by Klyamkin and Migranyan failed to arouse even half of the scandal and outrage that was provoked by *Vekhi*.[3] Those who wrote replies were mainly journalists and political scientists, as though the matter did not affect the creative intelligentsia. Does this not indicate that a very large number of members of our intelligentsia have already undergone a definitive transformation into intellectuals? In the current situation, unfortunately, even this is not the worst possible interpretation of events.

The rejection of democratic ideals and of the concept of 'the good of the people', which was critical for the old intelligentsia whatever its party affiliations and which was still current in the 1960s, means in practice the rejection by the intelligentsia of its special place in society as the collective bearer of moral-political values and the inevitable displacement of the *intelligent* by the Western intellectual, though without Western levels of education and competence. Having ceased to be an intelligentsia in the Russian sense of the word, and without really having become intellectuals of the Western type, we risk losing ourselves without gaining an identity in exchange.

Fortunately, the situation is not quite so hopeless. The complaints of the liberals and of the official apparatchiks at the rapid growth of 'left radicalism' are far from groundless. The new generation of the intelligentsia, like their predecessors of a hundred or of thirty years ago, are discovering that the system which is in formation has no place for them. For the moment the revolt of the new generation is better expressed in rock music than in literature (though paradoxically, the literary quality of rock lyrics has suddenly become unexpectedly high).

Who the important new literary figures will be still remains to be discovered. But the new political slogans are already obvious. It was precisely the young intelligentsia who formed the framework for the rapidly gathering forces of the democratic movement, which must now arm itself with the traditional socialist principles of collective solidarity, self-management and social justice.

The renewal of the intelligentsia can undoubtedly provide a powerful impulse for the development of literature, though even in the case of the final disappearance of the intelligentsia, literature would not vanish. But this would be a different literature. Most likely, the force of cultural tradition is strong enough to ensure that this tradition will be reborn under new conditions, though it is very difficult to predict in precisely what forms. So far, the outlines of the new political tendencies have been emerging much more clearly than the features of the new creative trends.

In any case, a whole generation will have to elapse before the present crisis is overcome. The final choice between intellectuals and the intelligentsia has not yet been made, and it is entirely possible that today we are seeing not the death of the intelligentsia but, on the contrary, the beginning of a new stage in its history. However, this rebirth is only possible if we clearly recognize our socio-cultural role and once again display the capacity which traditionally has distinguished the intelligentsia: the capacity to swim against the stream.

Farewell to 'Westernism'

The prevailing ideology of the official press, saturating both the declarations of the government and the monologues of opposition activists, is 'Westernism'. The urge to orient oneself to a different culture and to copy ready-made models, combined with a contemptuous and at times aggressively fearful relationship to one's own people and history, is not only one of the signs of ideological provincialism, but also a characteristic manifestation of the very 'Asiatic barbarism' which these people are supposedly about to eradicate.

The point is that the 'Westernizing idea' has from the very beginning contained insoluble contradictions. It is far from accidental that it was during the eighteenth century – the period of cutting 'a window on to Europe' – that serfdom in Russia flourished to its fullest extent. The 'Westernizing tradition', embodied in concrete political decisions, was transformed into an ideological justification for the anti-popular actions of the authorities. In actual fact political Westernism has always been directed towards ensuring that an 'advanced', privileged, 'enlightened' minority would have the conditions for a 'civilized' life and 'civilized' consumption on the European model. At the same time it has also presupposed the establishment of an economic structure corresponding as closely as possible to the Western standards of the time (Peter the Great built factories and organized a navy, Stalin established a machine-building industry, while the present-day Westernizers dream of computers). The only problem is that in the conditions of a backward country rapid solutions to these problems have only been possible through intensifying the oppression of the 'backward' majority.

Western society took shape without any need for such a concept as 'Westernization'. For any Western society progress involved an affirmation of the national culture, not a rejection of it. The historically developed state structures of Europe and the USA, with all their strengths and weaknesses, were not forced on to society from above or from outside; they were the product of the natural development of society itself.

Westernization demands a rejection of one's own identity and the condemnation of one's own history – not just any single stage of it, but in essence the whole tradition, the whole history, everything which does not conform to the model of 'normal' (that is, Western) development as the supporters of this kind of 'progress' present it. In practice this denies the central element in the Western tradition: its popular character. Democracy means the power of the majority; that is, the last word always belongs to the people, to the masses, not to the 'elite'. It is precisely this principle which is unacceptable to the Westernizers, who in the final accounting have always relied on the old Byzantine principle according to which power in society must be concentrated in the hands of the possessors of 'knowledge', or as it has been put in more recent times, the 'enlightened classes'.

The contradiction between the democratic ideas which have come to us from Western Europe on the one hand, and the logic of Russian Westernism on the other, was already apparent to the Russian intelligentsia in the nineteenth century. In essence, the general interest which the intelligentsia had in the ideas of socialism was a response to the spiritual downfall of Westernism. However, today's Westernizers cite 'the collapse of socialist ideas', the worldwide historical triumph of capitalism and so forth. To be a socialist in Soviet society, where a totalitarian regime took cover behind socialist phraseology, was always difficult, but it became especially difficult when the old propaganda machine, kept in reserve for decades, tried to profit from the collapse of the ideology it once propagated, and preached the values of the 'free market', citing its own example as proof of the worthlessness of socialism.

Westernizing ideology in its pure form has never before enjoyed such influence in Russia. And it has never before been as anti-democratic, as dangerous, as now in the 1990s.

The social character of Westernism in Russia, as in the countries of the Third World, is fairly obvious. The reasons for Westernist illusions lie not merely in the provincialism, backwardness, incompetence and 'non-Western character' of a significant part of the 'enlightened elite', but also in its marginal nature, its isolation from society, its declassed character, and in its lack of any clear and recognized social role.

However, the problem has assumed various forms in different epochs. The Westernist orientation of the regime today is a clear testimony to its crisis and marginalization. The state authorities were just as marginalized in post-Petrine Russia, in the times of Anna Ioannovna, Anna Leopoldovna, Yelisaveta Petrovna and even Catherine the Great. These were regimes isolated from society, profoundly hostile to the majority of the people and to the people's traditions and history.

Sadly, it must be said that Stalin's regime was not marginalized; at that time society itself was declassed, marginalized and atomized. The regime was the only organized, unifying force in the country. In this, and not in the terror, lay the astonishing stability of the Stalinist system despite its catastrophic failures. The terror was meant not only to intimidate the population, but above all to disorganize society, to transform it into a marginalized mass.

Towards the end of the twentieth century Russian society, having more or less recovered from the shock of the Stalinist terror, confronts a regime which is less and less able to prove its right to exist, its raison d'être. Naturally, such a weakened regime can no longer inspire real dread, but neither can it become legitimate and democratic. As in the past, it remains anti-popular. Only now, this anti-popular character is expressed differently. It manifests itself as social irresponsibility.

This marginality is also characteristic of that part of the intellectual elite which is most closely linked with the pinnacles of government. In this case irresponsibility in the conduct of socio-political affairs is transformed into cultural irresponsibility. If those in power conduct irresponsible reforms, trying in one way and another to restore or strengthen their position, the intellectuals of the new type call on the population to trust in the benefits of the chosen path, to break with their own history and culture, traditions and experience. Whatever devices the supporters of the new authoritarian liberalism might resort to, the true essence of their position becomes increasingly obvious. It is not concern for popular welfare or economic progress, but simply the irresponsible social egoism of a part of the middle strata, out to form a political bloc with part of the old nomenklatura in order to divide up state property. It is a deal between thieves, of the most commonplace kind.

Society is gradually facing up to reality. Ever greater numbers of people, including members of the middle strata, are beginning to feel that the new ideology is a vulgar fraud. But 'what is to be done'? That is the eternal question for Russians. And answering it today is much more difficult than in the past.

Notes

1. When in 1990 the Moscow joint venture PUICO republished the book by the right-wing socialist S. P. Melgunov, *The Red Terror in Russia, 1918–1923*, the authors of the afterword, A. Daniel and N. Okhotin, took the risk of mentioning the need to conduct 'serious academic research' not only on the Red but also on the White Terror (p. 204). Unfortunately, no one as yet has undertaken such research. The ruling circles of today, like those of twenty years ago, simply have no need of it, while the academic intelligentsia prefer to give interviews and write propaganda articles.
2. *Izvestiya*, 28 September 1990.
3. It should be noted that the scandal erupted around a totally different matter. When in the journal *Gorizont* ('Horizon', 1990, no. 5), I published an article entitled 'Intellectuals Versus the Intelligentsia', which forms the basis of the present chapter, I unexpectedly found that in intellectual circles I had acquired the status almost of an 'enemy of society'.

3

Political Mosaic:
Left and Right

'Support the forces of the right!' urges a speaker at a Popular Front meeting in Luzhniki. 'The press has taken an incomprehensible turn to the left,' complains a writer of the 'village' school in a newspaper. 'First the right wing tries to pressure us, then the left, but we will stick firmly to our own course,' a state functionary promises his audience.

In conditions of intensified political struggle the concepts of 'right' and 'left' have become an integral part of our daily life. They are used everywhere, appropriately and inappropriately. Attempts are sometimes made in samizdat journals to give a precise definition to these terms. For example, Dmitry Shubin declares categorically that Western leftists 'are totally different from ours', and argues that analogies here are out of place.[1] The Polish social activist Adam Michnik, until recently a 'dissident' but now a member of the Sejm, insists that the terms 'left' and 'right' should not be used at all, since they contradict the realities of Eastern Europe. But this is easier said than done, since a language has rules of its own. What is it that forces us continually to use these terms, which came to us from an 'alien' political civilization and another epoch?

'The terminological confusion is complete,' wrote the eminent jurist and political scientist B. P. Kurashvili in 1990. Mayakovsky describes the situation accurately: 'The street writhes without a tongue, it has nothing with which to shout or speak.' But in fact the street had two words at its disposal, 'Bastards!' and 'Tripe!' The street, one may assume, used these in their appropriate sense. But Soviet commentators who have a significantly greater store of learned terms at their disposal, use a great many of them without their proper meaning. This is partly out of ignorance and partly intentional. Records for absurdity are being set through the use of the words 'left' and 'right' in their opposite senses. The word 'left' is used for any positive reference to oneself. Those who call themselves 'leftists' include champions of the recapitalization of Soviet society, that is the kind of 'progressives' and 'revolutionaries' who are bringing about the abolition of socialism and the return of capitalism, though capitalism of a new variety (these people are in fact genuine radicals, but radicals of the right).[2]

This tangle of concepts is being lifted from propaganda sketches into articles which have pretensions to being scholarly. The sociologists L. Byzov and G. Gurevich attempt in all seriousness to classify Soviet political currents under such headings as 'Westernizers', 'statists', 'social democrats', 'left populists', 'right populists', 'greens' and so on,[3] mixing up quite different cultural and political concepts in the one heap. From their descriptions it emerges that in their view right-wing populists include supporters of social justice and collectivism – that is, of everything which international political science has always termed left populism. Their description of the views of 'left populists' would easily lead one to believe that they were talking about social democrats (supporters of a mixed economy, of softening the contradictions of the market with the help of state regulation and so forth). Those who are described as social democrats are people who, while speaking out in favour of a free market, nonetheless acknowledge that taxes and state bodies have a certain role to play in the economy; that is, supporters of Thatcher and Reagan, right-wing liberals and conservatives. The 'Westernizers' are partisans of the most savage variety of capitalism who do not recognize themselves as such, and who consequently reject the principles on the basis of which contemporary 'civilized' capitalism has been constructed in the West. And so on, in the same vein.

All of these types actually exist, along with dozens and hundreds of others. The confusion of concepts, the absence of the most elementary understanding of the outside world and of the criteria accepted there, the general muddle-headedness – all this is completely normal for a society after decades of cultural isolationism and the rule of totalitarian propaganda. But a sociology which tries to construct a logical system on the basis of this tangle simply succeeds in turning itself into one more among the multitude of symptoms of political chaos. In order to understand the surrounding chaos one needs first of all to create some sort of elementary order inside one's own head.

Difficulties in handling political concepts do not only afflict us, nor are they confined to our own period. In journalist Anthony Sampson's *A New Anatomy of Britain* I cam across the following passage:

> From the English point of view it has always been difficult to say who is on the left. In essence, this term derives from a continental concept which has its origins in the French National Convention of 1789. . . . The concept of

the 'left' began spreading in Britain only at the beginning of the present century, and it has never been possible to apply it fully to the Labour Party. Various attempts have been made to explain the difference between the right and left more precisely. Here are some of the peculiarities which from time to time have been used to characterize them:

Leftists	Rightists
Nationalization	Private enterprise
Changes	Traditions
Equality	Elitism
Sympathy	Harshness
Tolerance	Discipline
'Doves'	'Hawks'
Democracy	Aristocracy
State regulation	Freedom for private initiative[4]

In my view three components are missing from this classification. First, in the twentieth century leftists have traditionally proclaimed their ideology to be socialism (although the interpretations given to the concept of socialism can be profoundly different). Second, a distinguishing characteristic of the left movement in the West has always been the workers' struggle for democratic participation in running the economy. Leftists, in other words, attack the rights of property, and it matters nothing whether the property concerned is that of a private firm or of the state. In both cases limitations on the rights of property are indispensable if democratization is to go ahead.

Of course, it is not only left parties that have used the slogan of socialism. In the 1930s and 1940s in certain Western circles it was fashionable to say that 'we are all socialists now.' Those who flirted with socialist terminology included liberals, fascists, and nationalist figures in Latin America whose bourgeois character would be difficult to doubt. Like any vogue word, the term 'socialist' suffered abuse. But the ideology of the left always embodied an understanding of socialism which unfailingly included the predominance of society over the state, firm social guarantees for workers – guarantees, not sops bestowed through the goodwill of the generous authorities – and democratic control over production.

From this point of view Stalinism has always fitted uneasily into the traditions of the left movement. At one time Stalinist ideologues generally avoided using the term 'left', but in the periods of the United

Front and the Union of Left Forces, when it was indispensable to unite with the socialists, they referred to themselves as part of the 'left camp'. It is very likely that in their own way these ideological contradictions reflected the internal contradiction of Stalinism, which fought against 'restricted bourgeois democracy' in the name of workers' interests while simultaneously denying workers their democratic rights.

Third and finally, 'leftists' are those who act on the side of the workers against the ruling classes and the oligarchy. This is the main criterion and the one that determines all the others. If you find it difficult to understand 'who is on the left and who on the right', it means that the movement of the masses themselves is still not developed, and that the final delineation of class forces in society has not yet emerged.

Let us return to Sampson. In the 1960s, he writes, confusion arose 'in defining what should really be considered leftist.' Both of the main parties in Great Britain held similar views on all the basic questions of national life. Compromise ruled. Alas, Anthony Sampson's observations on Britain in the 1960s and 1970s no longer applied by the 1980s. With the advent of Mrs Thatcher, no one could doubt that there was a difference between left and right in Britain. The polarization of forces proceeded, and the conflicting camps clearly defined their positions. The reforms of the Conservative government, which was pursuing a radical right-wing course, provoked a leftward shift in the opposition. The struggles between miners and police during the 1984 strike showed clearly and concretely that the struggle was not one of abstract ideals but of living interests.

If even in Britain, with its long-established political culture, the question of what was 'left' and 'right' could evoke confusion, it is not hard to see what a conceptual mess prevails in Russia following the totalitarian experiment which has been conducted on us. A totalitarian regime by definition cannot be either left-wing or right-wing. It always claims to stand on positions of the general interest and the highest good. It cuts across biases to the 'left' or 'right', without, however, declaring itself to be the centre. For it to make any such self-definition would signify that some other position, distinct from the official one, might exist in society. A totalitarian regime cannot occupy any part of the political spectrum, since it itself replaces the entire spectrum. Its logic is that of universal equilibrium. If a 'right-wing' deviation were to arise somewhere, then for the sake of symmetry a 'left-wing' one would have to be discovered and annihilated. The logic of totalitarianism is summed up in the wisdom of the camps: 'A step to the left or a step to the right will be considered an attempt at escape. The guard will shoot without warning!'

Of course, a totalitarian regime can use either 'left' or 'right' terminology, depending on which 'works' better in the given situation. As a rule, however, the political language of totalitarianism is mixed. Stalin spoke both as the inheritor of the revolution and as the embodiment of the idea of the Russian state. He cited proletarian principles and insisted on national priorities. He declared proudly that revenge had been exacted for the defeat inflicted by Japan on the Russian Empire.

In any case, the concepts of 'right' and 'left' acquire meaning only when a political struggle erupts, and when the elementary conditions arise for political pluralism. Under the conditions of totalitarianism in our country there could not be a place for an opposition, and therefore there were no politics – understood as competition between different political groupings. It was only in the 1960s that civil society began to take shape here, that various groups and currents arose which were not under the control of the authorities. It was no accident that it was precisely at this time that people here first began to talk about the 'left' and 'right'. Finally, in the 1980s political life began to 'thaw'. From somewhere (perhaps out of clandestinity?) there began to appear an extremely wide range of groups, from anarcho-syndicalists to monarchists. And so, naturally, there arose confusion.

In different cultures the terms 'left' and 'right' have a quite different emotional impact. In France rightists are not ashamed to call themselves rightists. In Russia, by contrast, the term 'left' is seen as particularly attractive. Leftists speak out against the authorities, they establish an opposition, and in a country which has not known political freedoms, this in and of itself is widely considered a great benefit. But it does not follow that any opposition constitutes a left wing.

A great many of the popular ideologues and political figures who formed the core first of the Moscow and then of the interregional group of deputies cannot in any sense be characterized as leftists. Their positions are those of classical liberalism, and in the spectrum of contemporary political life they clearly make up the centre. The fact that liberals should number themselves among the 'leftists' is nothing new for Russia; this was also the case with the Constitutional Democratic Party in the period of the 1905 revolution. Many of their slogans sound very radical, but if you look closely at the programmes and political practice of Russian liberals it is easy to see that their positions have changed little in eighty-odd years.

Dreams of a Bright (Capitalist) Future

The demands that everything possible be transferred into private hands and that market relations should everywhere be substituted for planning does not in any way undermine the overall positions of the ruling circles. What is occurring is merely a redistribution of power and privileges within these ruling groups. For the mass of the population, who are being allotted the role of hired workers, these changes will bring few or no improvements. Whether the suggested market reforms will raise the efficiency of the economy as a whole is debatable; the experience of Yugoslavia, Hungary and Poland indicates that in conditions of structural crisis such policies have nothing good to offer. But in any case it is clear that the liberal strategy must produce a rapid deterioration in the already far from wonderful living standards of the poorest strata of the population, together with intensified exploitation of the workforce and a rise in unemployment, which the supporters of the reforms now discuss quite openly. Even now, one can observe the enrichment of a small group of 'dynamic people'. The outlook is clear: power is to be exchanged for money, and money for power. Bureaucratic privileges which are illegal from the point of view of society are to be exchanged for 'legal' ones that have been earned and paid for.

The freedom of private initiative only means freedom for those with money. And who has money in our present society? Those same privileged strata who so loudly condemn our fashionable ideologues. Those who have money are the apparatchiks, the mafia and their relatives and friends. What is at issue here is not the restoration of capitalism, which is so frightening to those who are jealous of the good name of totalitarianism; the social groupings listed above are not even remotely capable of 'building developed capitalism' in our homeland. A civilized capitalism is possible only in the presence of a civilized bourgeoisie, whose formation in the West took more than three hundred years. However much we talk about the rich life in Sweden, and repeat interminably Lenin's formula that socialism is a society of 'civilized co-operators', our 'co-operators' (who in reality are small- and medium-scale private entrepreneurs) will not become civilized, and the Soviet economy will not become like that of Scandinavia. A small number of forward-looking co-operatives, which strive to master new technology, are organized on democratic principles and are conscious of their responsibility to society, cannot qualitatively change the situation, and will only succeed once again in demonstrating the barbarity and anti-democratic character of the others.

Under the real conditions which exist in our country an injection of capitalist methods can mean only a restructuring of relations within the privileged minority, while the basic characteristics of the existing system remain. It is hard to view such developments as a path to democracy. Our first experiences with co-operatives showed that the overwhelming majority of the population not only failed to relate to them with particular enthusiasm, but demanded bluntly that they be shut down. It is not hard to see what would be the fate of the liberal economic reforms if this depended on the will of the majority.

This situation explains the strange timidity and inconsistency shown by the liberals whenever they address political questions. They insist on sweeping freedoms, but are reluctant to assume the role of an opposition; they criticize the government on specific points, but are unwilling to suggest alternatives; in theory they support free trade unions, but in practice they call for an end to strikes and for all questions to be submitted to the 'parliamentary' organs of the Supreme Soviet, which not long ago they were describing as 'Stalinist-Brezhnevite'. In actual fact, the present semi-democratic organs and procedures are well suited to the liberal project. Consequently, the liberals are trying to perfect and rationalize them, not to replace them with new, democratic ones. The most recent period has seen an increasing number of authors speaking openly of the need for a strong authoritarian regime if the reforms are to succeed. The warm reception which the liberal public gave the article by Igor Klyamkin and Andranik Migranyan, now the chief ideologues of 'enlightened authoritarianism', was far from accidental. When Klyamkin and Migranyan argued in *Literaturnaya Gazeta* that the reforms which they proposed would not be accepted by the people and could not be implemented without a 'firm hand', they were absolutely right. Nevertheless, they did not acknowledge the anti-popular and anti-democratic character of their position, and faithfully repeated the traditional Stalinist schema: for the good of the people and democracy, the rights of the people must be restricted. Whether the people want our shining future or not, we will drive them there. This market Stalinism is the natural continuation and development of 'classic' Stalinism under the new conditions.

History is thus being repeated, with the liberals of the end of the century behaving vis-à-vis the existing system in exactly the same way as the liberals of the past acted towards tsarism. This resemblance seems at first glance to be all the more striking in that the conservatives of our day are so different from those of the past. Although in both cases the conservative forces rested on a bureaucracy with all its specific peculiarities, in old Russia there also existed a landed aristocracy and a large bourgeoisie. The present-day conservatives clearly have nothing of the bourgeois about them. They plead proletarian values, although they view real initiatives by the masses as 'riots' and 'insupportable declines in discipline'.

One should remember that most of the 'classic' Russian liberals were not bourgeois either. They were above all members of the privileged elite intelligentsia, part of the stratum of industrial managers, and enlightened officials of the state administration. In other words, they were from the same levels which provide support for liberalism today. The liberals of the early years of the century, like their modern counterparts, saw that the position of their colleagues in Western society was more prosperous and secure, and so without being capitalists themselves, and without preparing to apply themselves directly to the principal tasks of 'building capitalism', they dreamt of setting the country on the Western path of development. The only way this transition could be achieved in the absence of a developed bourgeois class was if the regime implanted new social relations from above, by methods that were anything but democratic. The main difference between 'classic' and contemporary Russian liberalism lies in the fact that at the beginning of the century the country possessed a small group of civilized bourgeois, whereas now there are only the eminently uncivilized co-operators and mafiosi.

An analysis of the social base of present-day Russian liberalism shows that its main support is among the 'middle levels'. In their nature, their mode of life and, most importantly, in their place within society the middle levels in Eastern Europe differ substantially from those of the West. First, and as noted earlier, they are relatively heterogeneous. They include workers in the retail trade, growing fat on shortages; the uppermost levels of the state apparatus in science and the economy; and the cream of the intelligentsia, the artistic and scientific elite. In the West the formation of the middle strata occurred in a more or less organic fashion during the process of transition from 'classical capitalism' to 'neocapitalism'. The boundaries between the propertied classes and the dispossessed grew less rigid; the role of state intervention in the economy expanded, as did the importance of technological innovations. Power became less concentrated; democratization went ahead, together with rises in the standard of living and the simultaneous growth of the role of hired labour in the non-productive sphere. The old petty bourgeoisie disappeared; in its place arose new middle strata, more numerous and more up-to-date, which became the backbone of the new capitalist society.

In the USSR and Eastern Europe, as in the countries of the Third World, the middle strata did not acquire such a key role in production or in the social structure. The predominance in these countries of traditional industrial technologies and the existence of rigid bureaucratic hierarchies excluded any possibility of the middle levels being consolidated into a homogeneous social group.

At the same time the development of society gave birth to middle levels in the East just as in the West. Their development could often be described as hypertrophic. The numbers of high-placed scientific workers and all-powerful 'responsible individuals' and bosses in science and production even appear to have exceeded society's needs, especially if one considers the wretched results of their practical activity, and the extremely poor training which specialists received. In Russia, unlike the West, workers in the sphere of services and the retail trade became the most privileged sector of the middle levels. The constant shortages of goods and services that arose from the weak development of the consumer sphere placed these people in a unique position. For us, commerce and corruption have become synonyms. Hatred for workers in the sphere of trade has become a characteristic feature of the ideology of the masses. Meanwhile, members of these circles have been able to enrol their children in the most prestigious educational institutions as well as to forge links with the artistic world and with the most diverse levels of the system of government. Corruption has eaten away at the middle classes, at the same time as it has united and consolidated them.

Thus, for all the diversity of the middle strata – hairdressers, technicians, writers, managers of large enterprises, mafiosi, workers in trade and sportsmen and women – something has drawn them together: above all, a similar level of income and, as a consequence, a similar way of life based on a single standard of consumption. This is not only a matter of the quantity of goods consumed or money spent, but of similar access to similar goods which are missing from the shops. Their equal identification with the 'Western way of life' was seen first of all on the screens of the cinemas showing American war films and French comedies. This standard of consumption has turned out to be strikingly persistent, even surviving experience of the real West. The lists of purchases by Soviet tourists abroad are astonishingly uniform.[5] The tourists all exchanged something, sold things to one another, imitated one another, and tried not to lag behind.

At the beginning of the 1980s the video tape recorder became symbolic of the desirable standard to reach. An approximately equal level of access to goods in short supply has created a situation of equal possibilities and has given birth to uniform social orientations. In this melting-pot of the new consumer world general values are being formed, and along with them, a general ideology.

For a long time the level of consumption remained the principal unifying factor, but in the perestroika period the Law on Co-operation established a number of organizational structures. It was precisely the middle levels who were best able to form co-operatives. They had qualifications and a certain degree of expertise, but what was most important, it was only members of the middle levels who had significant financial means, which gave them a measure of independence. They also had a developed system of links with the apparatus, without which the formation of co-operatives in a bureaucratically corrupted society was inconceivable. The co-operative sector united the middle levels economically; here all its 'detachments' were represented, from the mafia to the creative elite.

At the same time, consumption continued to play a key role in the social consolidation of the middle strata, and consequently in the formation of their ideology. This explains a great deal. Why, for example, in the 1950s, when immediately after the death of Stalin the first opposition movements appeared in Eastern Europe, were they almost never 'Westernist'? To cite the discrediting of socialism in the Stalin epoch is to explain little, since in the final analysis the horrors of Stalinism should have been much more effective in repelling people from the concept of socialism than the stagnation of the Brezhnev years. In crushing the Prague Spring the Brezhnev regime shattered the illusions of the 'liberal communists' who had believed in a gradual democratization from above within the framework of the system. Nevertheless, the consolidation of 'Westernizing' pro-capitalist sentiments in the intelligentsia and society coincided with the rapid growth of the middle strata in the 1970s, and this was no accident.

Disappointment with the slogans of socialism was natural after decades of totalitarian-bureaucratic rule, during which millions of people had perished and the economy had been brought to complete collapse. But from a certain point the leaders of the opposition began to cherish and carefully cultivate this disappointment. The social base of the opposition was changing. In formal terms, the intelligentsia continued to play the leading role. But the intelligentsia of the 1950s differed strikingly from the intellectuals of the end of the 1970s. The former lived side by side with workers in communal apartments; their children went to the same schools, and their wives stood in the same queues. The latter already belonged to a privileged minority, alienated from power, but not from material benefits.

The Western-oriented standard of consumption of the new middle strata gave birth to generally 'Westernized' social ideals. The 'Westernizers', the sociologists L. Byzov and G. Gurevich state vaguely, are 'most often encountered among the intelligentsia and workers in the commercial sector'.[6] The essence of this 'Westernism' consists in the effort to form a structure to guarantee as far as possible the stability of this type of consumption for the social strata in question.

In Western Europe and America, however, the structure of consumption is determined ultimately by the structure of the economy. In the East, an attempt is being made to adapt the economic structures to a ready-made, borrowed model of consumption which historically was developed in the West.

If one reads the works of the ideologues closely, it becomes clear that what preoccupies them is the question of how to ensure consumption, and that the discussion revolves around a particular model of consumption by the middle strata. The fact that a considerable part of the population lives in quite different circumstances and has trouble making ends meet concerns them little. If someone is dissatisfied and looks like encroaching on the consumer paradise, the logic goes, a 'firm hand ' is needed to defend the 'progressive minority' from the mass of the unenlightened.

An indispensable component of the liberal project in Russia, now and in earlier times, has been the existence of a strong regime able to carry through important changes. Here the Russian liberal has always found a common language with the conservative. The problem is that today's conservatives, as a result of their changed social base, are relatively unreceptive to the idea of the Western road. Ideologues opposed to perestroika organized the United Front of Workers, trying to find support among the masses. In effect proclaiming themselves the opposition, they are trying to occupy the political space which logically should belong to the left.

The unofficial organizations which appeared throughout the country after 1987 presented a rich political spectacle. It was here that a large part of the left flank of our collective life was to be found. But the experience of the informal oganizations showed that many groups which were indisputably radical were not in the least leftist.

The concepts of 'radicalism' and 'conservatism' very often do not coincide with the labels 'left' and 'right'. In the first instance we find two types of approaches to our present-day reality, and in the second, two choices of values. An analogous situation exists in the West. The British Labour Party, despite its unquestioned adherence to the values of the left camp, has in particular periods of its history shown a striking conservatism, including a complete incapacity to change anything in society or in its own practice. This predetermined the party's catastrophic defeat in 1979, from which the British socialists to this day have been unable to recover. At the same time as the left has become increasingly conservative and pragmatic, the right has become ideologized and radicalized. The Thatcher government was indisputably one of the most radical in postwar Britain. And, unquestionably, the most right-wing.

The political organizations which arose in our country during 1987 and 1988 were also clearly divided into right-wing and left-wing, although the critical question at that time was their attitude to the existing system, and, consequently, people were concerned mainly with the radicalism of each group's tactics, rather than with the character of its strategic goals. As a result, the anarchists of the 'Commune' group figured among the 'moderates', since they sought to act within the framework of the current laws, making use of the legal possibilities, while certain liberal groups aroused suspicions of 'extremism'.

The majority of the leftists in Russia united in 1988 around the Popular Front movement, while the rightists found their refuge in the Democratic Union. Thanks to the consistent anti-communism of its leaders the Democratic Union in many respects appeared more radical than the Moscow or Yaroslavl Popular Fronts. Also important was the fact that by declaring itself a party, the Democratic Union excluded any possibility of Communist Party members joining in its activity. As later developments showed, it was by no means the case that CPSU members always held left-wing views. As a rule, however, they adopted more moderate tactics with regard to the system to which they were connected in one way or another through their party membership.

Like the organizers of the Popular Front, the founders of the Democratic Union tried to avoid rigid ideological formulas in their programmatic documents and gave prominence to general democratic slogans. Nevertheless, the Democratic Union formed itself along the lines of a typical right-wing party, inspired by the values of private entrepreneurship and free competition. (Among the activists of this movement, belief in an ideal society that has already been constructed in the West is just as absolute as the faith in Red Russia held by Western Stalino-Communists in the 1930s.) On the other hand the Russian Popular Front, which raised the banner of self-government, can unquestionably be seen as belonging to the left camp, though this movement was not in the least homogeneous.

Each camp and each grouping possesses its own 'moderates' and 'radicals'. Psychologically these trends can have a great deal in common, even though their ideological positions are incompatible. A hankering after confrontation with the authorities and an inclination to call demonstrations on any pretext whatever, are characteristics which the most radical members of the Moscow Popular Front shared with activists of the Democratic Union. But ideologically the radicals in the Moscow Popular Front were furthest of all from the leaders of the Democratic Union; as a rule they were principled socialists, often Marxists. It is enough to compare the paper *Nashe Delo*, published by radicals from the Moscow Popular Front, with the Democratic Union publication *Svobodnoe Slovo* to see the incompatibility of these two types of radicalism. The overall relationship between radicalism and conservatism on the left and right is set out in the diagram.

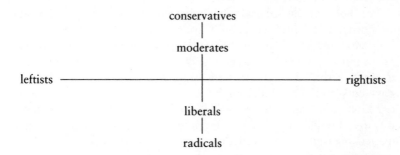

In the mid-1980s, when the key questions being decided were whether important changes would take place in our country, and whether these would be profound enough really to 'reconstruct' society, it was precisely the conflict between conservatives and 'progressives' that was thrust to the forefront. All of the proponents of change formed a sort of single liberal-radical-left bloc, giving little thought to the contradictions among themselves. But from the moment when the changes began to come into effect and the process of breaking down the old structures began, the contradictions between the diverse values and interests in the original progressive camp emerged and quickly became acute.

The leftists, for example, spoke out in favour of educational reforms which would be aimed at giving everyone equal access to a diverse, high-quality but free education. Their goal was a system of instruction which would give pupils a free choice while observing the principle of complete equality of rights. This would involve various forms of educational self-management and would require a radical reform of the entire state educational system. The liberals, by contrast, put their stake on co-operative (and in the longer term, private) schools for especially gifted or wealthy children, co-operative kindergartens, and the development of elite educational institutions.

The liberals had an analogous approach to health care. The principle is simple: quality services for those who can pay. Suggestions that the prices will be relatively affordable do not change anything in essence. For one thing prices can rise, and for another, if paid health care is added to paid education, if housing costs are set in accordance with the 'free market', and if free services are replaced by paid ones in order to make service areas which now depend on subsidies 'commercially viable' – in short, if the socio-economic reforms urged by liberals throughout the world are consistently implemented – then it can be seen that not only quality education but also elementary health care will become luxuries for the few.

The hero of the liberal ideologues in our country is Stanislav Feodorov, a talented surgeon who has turned his activity into a brilliantly organized and profitable business which has been proposed as the model for a new system of health care. It does not seem to occur to anyone that the very fact of establishing a connection between payments and the quality of health care represents a fundamental rejection of humanist principles. Health is not a privilege, or a commodity to be bought or picked out. From the point of view of leftists it is an inalienable right of the individual, and the quality of the medical care one receives should not depend on the amount of money in one's purse. The market provides the possibility of choosing between commodities. But turning health into a commodity means treating the worth of the human individual with total contempt.

The right to choose one's doctor should not be limited by one's financial means. The old system of social guarantees was inefficient and bureaucratized, providing huge scope for directorial arbitrariness (I can give or I can refuse to give) and for corruption; its crisis obliges us to struggle for a radical reform in this area. But reform can proceed in various directions. Of course, it would be simpler to follow the road urged by the liberals – that is, to create special, highly efficient and costly medical and educational services for the rich, while leaving the provisions for the majority more or less as they are (in practice, these provisions would deteriorate still further, since all of the more skilled specialists would gravitate to the privileged establishments). Taking this path would be much simpler than trying to create a system that guaranteed equal provision for all, and would be much safer and more convenient for the traditional apparatus. No one would encroach on their power. The liberals do not in fact aim at destroying the system of rule by the apparatus, but at carving out 'special zones' for themselves within this system, just like the 'special zones' for foreign capital which are being created within the economy. Naturally, to the extent that the liberal wave has grown, the ambitions of the opposition elite have increased as well. Nevertheless their approach has not changed. The majority of the population are to remain beyond the bounds of the 'special zone' precisely because this is how the well-being of the chosen few within it is to be guaranteed.

In this case the interests of the chosen few and of the bureaucratic circles coincide. Just like the mixed enterprises, special economic zones and so on, these 'radical' measures are in fact crutches for the old system, structures created to maintain its viability in new conditions and to serve as a substitute for more profound and thorough democratic changes.

The programme of limited liberal reforms within the framework of the system involves relatively few risks for the old bureaucracy. (It should be noted that the more radical the market reform which is proposed, and the clearer the orientation towards the 'advanced experience' of capitalism, the greater becomes the need for a 'firm hand', and consequently for the old apparatus.) This liberal programme has also been carefully worked out, something which should not seem surprising. Marx and Engels were of course exaggerating when they said that the dominant ideas in any society were the ideas of the ruling class. But it is also beyond question that the privileged strata, including those in our country, always enjoy great advantages in formulating their political strategy. Throughout the first three years of the Gorbachev period the liberal circles fully controlled the mass information media. Naturally, they also dominated the upper levels of official science.

The dominance of liberalism was an inevitable stage in the transition from obligatory official dogma to genuine ideological pluralism. In this respect liberalism played an important positive role, serving to shatter the original stereotypes. It was precisely within the framework of the united liberal-progressive bloc that leftist ideas were originally formed. But as the situation changed, the liberal ideological monopoly became increasingly dangerous. As the leftists took their distance from the liberals, they lost access to the mass information media just as trust in the newspapers and television was rising sharply. Under conditions of glasnost the position of dissidents who lacked access to the press and television became in a sense even more painful than it had been earlier.

The liberal monopoly in the press led to a rapid devaluation of language. For centuries in Russia everyone had believed in the might of the word. The persecutions suffered by writers, the reprisals against Pasternak, Grossman and Solzhenitsyn, people's heroic struggle to read their works, Bulgakov's famous statement that 'manuscripts do not burn', all bore witness to the fact that persecutors and persecuted alike believed in the power of the word. Now this faith has collapsed. In the course of three years glasnost succeeded in effacing age-old ideas. Grossman, Pasternak and Solzhenitsyn are printed, and nothing changes as a result. The belief in the power of the word has been supplanted by a phenomenon totally in the spirit of Western liberalism: repressive tolerance. One can voice dissident ideas, but mere words will not bring change. Only organization and action can alter people's lives.

Notes

1. In *Nevskie Zapiski*, 1989, no.5, a popular Moscow publicist even declared that what the Western world considered 'leftist' was 'rightist' in the USSR, and vice versa. One can, of course, use words in a wide variety of senses: their meaning is relative. But if in history and science certain meanings become established for particular terms, any attempt to rearrange these meanings or substitute them for one another is catastrophic. If what is called oxygen in America is called hydrogen in Russia, scientific research becomes simply impossible; the language of theory is destroyed, and everyone acquires the ability to overturn concepts as they think fit. This is what is happening today in our Russian political discussions.
2. B. P. Kurashvili, *Strana na rasput'e* ('The Country at the Crossroads'), Moscow 1990, p. 21.
3. *Argumenty i Fakty*, 1990, no. 7, p. 6.
4. A. Sampson, *The New Anatomy of Britain*, New York 1972.
5. V. Aksenov in his book *The Island of Crimea* provides a virtually complete list of the purchases which, it is suggested, need to be made in the West if the Soviet consumer standard of the beginning of the 1980s is to be regained. Before making a journey to Moscow the hero

> failed to buy double razor blades, colour film for mini-photos, flash-bulbs, jazz records, shaving cream, long socks, jeans – Oh, God! The eternal Soviet swearword, jeans! – T-shirts with logos, running shoes, women's boots, downhill skis, sound systems, skivvies, bras and panties, woollen pantihose, ivory hairpins, angora and cashmere sweaters, Alka-Seltzer tablets, power cables for taperecorders, paper napkins, talcum-powder for secluded spots, Scotch tape and Scotch whisky, tonic, gin, vermouth, ink for Parker and Mont Blanc pens, leather jackets, dictaphone cassettes, woollen underwear, sheepskin coats, winter boots, foldaway umbrellas, gloves, dried spices, kitchen calendars, tampons, flow-masters, coloured thread, lipstick, hi-fi apparatus, nail polish and nail polish remover – how this was underlined! – hair-bands, contraceptive pills and children's food, condoms and teats for babies' bottles, triple vaccines for dogs, a flea collar, air pistols, Monopoly games, electric switches and rheostats, coffee grinders, coffee urns, dark glasses, wall-mounted can openers, coloured stick-on veneers for tables, Polaroid cameras, car fire extinguishers, car cassette players, STP nozzles for autograse, gas cylinders for cigarette lighters and piezo-electric lighters, shower curtains with rings, quartz watches, halogen headlamps, knitted ties, *Vogue*, *Playboy*, *Downbeat*, suede leather, and any kind of food he could lay his hands on.

(*Iunost*, 1990, no. 2, p. 24)
6. *Argumenty i Fakty*, 1990, no. 7, p. 6.

4

A New Model of Democracy?
Populism

It is entirely natural that the liberals should have relied for their political impact on the official press, on speeches at various congresses and conferences, and on addressing documents to the authorities. Meanwhile the left, temporarily forced on to the sidelines, tried to establish its own alternative press (in the spirit of Lenin, newspapers are still 'collective organizers'), and to work in the mass movements. The popular fronts which arose in various Russian cities were the first manifestation of this tendency towards democratic self-organization. The political character of the fronts remained somewhat ill-defined. In many cases they did not take their distance from liberalism, and they lacked political experience and competent cadres. But all left movements have encountered such problems in the first stages of their development.

Many figures in the liberal camp immediately recognized a threat in the popular fronts that were springing up around Russia. *Moskovskie Novosti* published a series of articles attacking the Moscow Popular Front, and refused members the right of reply. The appearance of the Yeltsin movement aroused even greater concern in liberal circles. Yeltsin's speeches did not put forward a clear programme, and there was no single organization backing him. In many cases Yeltsin's demands echoed those of the liberals. Nevertheless, 'Yeltsinism' caused unease among the supporters of the liberal project, since the name of Yeltsin was drawing the masses on to the streets.

Even before the slogan of support for Yeltsin had given rise to a mass movement in Moscow and other cities, the term 'populism' had appeared in the newspapers. In the traditional political vocabulary this term had denoted socially heterogeneous mass movements without a clear programme or developed organizational structure, united by very general slogans or by the personality of the leader. Solidarity in Poland was a typical populist movement despite the predominance of workers within its ranks. The popular fronts in Russia and the Baltic republics were also populist in character. In place of a concrete programme they advanced general appeals for democracy, social justice and independence.

Paradoxically, the very unwillingness or inability of the Moscow Popular Front to become a consistently populist organization, together with the efforts of its 'socialist core' to formulate clear demands and a positive programme, meant that it remained relatively small (though during its periods of growth it developed according to the logic of populism, on the basis of the crowds attracted to its meetings by the radicalism of its speakers).

The mass populist movement in Moscow was linked to the name of Telman Gdlyan. Renowned for his struggle against corruption and the mafias, Detective Gdlyan easily managed to attract thousands of faithful followers who did not ask difficult questions about his economic programme.

Amid this wave of enthusiasm the populist leaders were easily elected to the Congress of People's Deputies in 1989. But once in congress they were not addressing mass meetings but an assembly of politicians, and they were obliged to discuss questions on which the mass meetings had never required them to develop firm views.

As a result of becoming deputies, the populists thus grew increasingly dependent on the liberals. Unable to develop their own ideological positions, they borrowed the alien ones that were being propagated through the mass media.

It is clear that the liberals did not achieve hegemony simply as a result of winning the support of popular figures such as Yeltsin and his circle for the ideas of 'private enterprise and the free market'. With their ability to block expression of other ideas in the newspapers and on television, the liberals were able effectively to influence the majority of the population and hence the social base of the populist leaders. Nevertheless, without the support of these leaders the liberals could not attract large numbers to their cause. Just as parliament was not the native element of the populist leaders, addressing crowds was not the favourite mode of expression of the advocates of liberalism.

From this point each of the two political groups was obliged to compensate for the inadequacies of the other. The socialists, grouped beneath the banner of the Moscow Popular Front, hoped that the liberal monopoly of the mass media would be balanced by populist control over the mass movement, and that with a certain equilibrium existing in the political life of the country the conditions would appear for the development of a genuine pluralism. In fact, the reverse happened. If in 1988 the spontaneously formed populist movements had formed a bloc with the socialist left, in more or less clear opposition to the liberals, in 1989 a single liberal-populist bloc was established, and the left found itself isolated.

The decisive stage in the formation of this bloc was marked by the elections to the Congress of People's Deputies and by the sittings of the congress. During the election campaign in Moscow, when thousands of people spontaneously took to the streets in support of Yeltsin who had been attacked by the official press, the Moscow Popular Front had been the only political organization able to profit from the crisis. Speakers from the front addressed meetings of many thousands of people at Luzhniki. At the end of the first meeting the crowd even broke into singing the 'Internationale'. Representatives of Moscow Tribune (a club of the liberal elite) and liberal deputies appeared here rather in the capacity of guests. But once the elections were over, the situation began to change. This process continued during the congress session.

The role played by the meetings at Luzhniki altered sharply. Initially they had provided a forum at which new, mainly left-wing social movements and rank-and-file voters from the most diverse corners of the country could express their views – which were ignored by both the conservative and liberal press – and could direct demands at politicians. By the end of the first congress session the meetings had become a place where liberal activists could meet with the masses and agitate among them. Liberal control of the press had been supplemented by control over the street.

For leftists, this reversal came as a complete surprise. In Moscow in the spring of 1989 the most prominent unofficial political organizations had been the Moscow Popular Front and the Democratic Union. As has already been noted, the first was dominated by socialists, but pursued reformist goals and employed relatively moderate tactics. The second mainly comprised right-wingers, on a basis of anti-communism and transition to a 'normal' capitalist society; ideologically, the Democratic Union formed the radical wing of the same liberal movement which dominated the mass media. But in the new context, neither radical liberals nor moderate leftists managed to achieve anything substantial.

The Moscow Popular Front was radicalized rather quickly, but since it was still mainly an organization of 'moderates', it found no alternative to giving 'critical support' to the liberal-populist bloc. Meanwhile, its criticisms were voiced in the context of theoretical discussion which made virtually no impact on the population; the official press did not publish these views, and support for them was manifested through the organization of meetings and demonstrations, participation in election campaigns and so forth. In this manner the Moscow Popular Front, despite its constantly emphasized socialist character, was forced in the final analysis to serve the liberal cause.

The only member of the Moscow Popular Front to be elected to the Congress of People's Deputies was Sergei Stankevich. He quickly became popular among television viewers and journalists. But unfortunately, from the time of his election Stankevich's political position became less and less distinguishable from those of other opposition figures. No longer an 'informal', he quickly dropped his links to the movement which had helped him mount the parliamentary platform. It would be unfair to lay the blame for this exclusively on Stankevich, who after all has remained one of the most left-wing among the new liberal politicians. The problem lay not only with him, but with the tactics which the Moscow Popular Front had chosen.

Ideologically the socialists were being forced further and further into isolation, and on the organizational level the ill-disciplined movement which was the Moscow Popular Front could not consolidate its gains. Judging from opinion polls the front's popularity had been steadily rising, but by the spring of 1990 the majority of leading activists of the popular fronts in Moscow and Leningrad had become deputies to the soviets, the growth in the ranks was no longer significant, and most importantly the organization's inability to formulate and pursue its own policies had become increasingly obvious. It is typical that in none of the soviets did the deputies who had taken part in the popular front movement even try to form their own fraction or group. Outwardly they were successful, but they had no strategic perspectives, and consequently their success was essentially equal to defeat.

The Moscow Popular Front's equivocal political positions meant that the organization not only failed to overcome the ideological divisions within its ranks, but that these even grew in intensity. The people who had joined the front in the spring and summer of 1989 had been attracted by the speeches of Popular Front activists in support of Yeltsin and the liberal deputies, and by the Luzhniki meetings, whose content and political significance by the end of the summer of 1989 were quite different from what they had been in the spring. Meanwhile, a ferment had begun among the front's activists. Many of them were moving to the right. The front's role as a junior partner in the liberal-populist bloc suited them perfectly. For the convinced socialists, the loss by the front of its original political character was traumatic. The organization's inability to transform itself into a left alternative to liberalism forced the socialists to consider establishing their own party.

The first step in this direction was the setting up within the Moscow Popular Front of the Moscow Committee of New Socialists. Soon analogous groups and committees began to arise in other cities as well, above all in centres such as Irkutsk, Samara and Leningrad where a more or less strong popular front movement had existed earlier.

The political failure of the Moscow Popular Front was not an exception. After the first session of the Congress of People's Deputies the popular fronts entered a period of crisis, and following the 1990 elections suffered a general collapse.

Nor was the Democratic Union able to boast of major political successes. The leaders of the Democratic Union sought at any cost to maintain the body's role as the most radical opposition organization, calling continually for a boycott of the elections. As a result the Democratic Union not only placed itself 'outside the game' at the very time when the majority of the Soviet population sincerely believed in the possibility of bringing about real change through electing 'honest and progressive deputies', but also deprived itself of any possibility of establishing links with official liberals who were closer to it in spirit. There was no real difference between the programmatic principles of the Democratic Union and the ideas of the 'official opposition' in the soviets, and as the liberal deputies sought to make an impression on the public, they resorted increasingly to anti-communist rhetoric in the style of the Democratic Union. But that organization in itself was quite superfluous to their needs. Politically, the liberals were oriented towards participation in elections, and radicals who called for boycotts could only impede this strategy.

It could be said that by the beginning of the 1990s all the movements and organizations which perestroika had called into existence had completely exhausted themselves. Populism had constituted a natural transitional stage in the formation of an organized left movement, just as the liberal-progressive bloc was indispensable for the transition from Brezhnevite ideological stagnation to pluralism. The instability of such formations was obvious. Warnings of the presence of a 'general enemy' in the shape of the bureaucracy allowed the supporters of different strategies to coexist only until it became obvious that a significant part of the 'progressive bloc' was less interested in defeating the bureaucracy than in reaching an accommodation with it. As the conservative mood intensified among the liberals and a section of the 'populist' leaders, the rank-and-file political activists were faced with a choice: whether to turn to the left or to the right.

The shift to political parties, which were now taking the place of broad coalitions, 'fronts' and mass movements with ill-defined ideologies and programmes consisting of general slogans, was a natural result of the increasing demarcation of political forces. Everything was changing before one's eyes. People who not long before had been jealous of their ideological orthodoxy began talking about pluralism. On Moscow's Pushkin Square, from which activists of the Democratic Union had once been driven by force, there appeared official placards in the best traditions of Stalinist propaganda but this time extolling the market and private property. The symbols of the new era were the MacDonalds Restaurant and the huge Coca-Cola sign now rising triumphantly above this same Pushkin Square.

Through a paradoxical turnabout the slogans of the Democratic Union, which for three years had been calling for the overthrow of 'Soviet totalitarianism', had become the slogans of the regime. Meanwhile the Democratic Union itself was in crisis. New parties and groups were arising, and seizing on fashionable ideas. The teachers of Marxism-Leninism were panic-stricken. What was happening? It was nothing like the collapse of totalitarianism; just as before, all the bosses were in their places, and despite the official declarations, events were not in the least reminiscent of revolution. A new political context had arisen, with democratic deputies forming majorities in the soviets in Moscow, Leningrad and a number of other cities. Democratic society had rejoiced at the election of Gavriil Popov, who earlier had drafted economic documents for the Brezhnevite Central Committee, to the post of president of the Moscow City Soviet, and then had been smitten with doubt on seeing Popov on the stand at the top of the mausoleum surrounded by members of the Politburo. Who were the 'ruling circles' and who the opposition?

The Power of the Soviets, or, From Chaos to Dictatorship

For the new type of liberal-populist politics that were developing in the country, at a certain stage the system of soviets became the ideal field of activity. The people elected to the soviets acquired enormous opportunities for canvassing their views, while the voters were completely deprived of any possibility of influencing the decisions that had been taken. To the degree that mass political parties were absent, the electors in essence voted blindly, without knowing the stance this or that candidate would adopt on specific questions. The politics of the 'new wave' included a preference for wooing voters with general phrases about democracy and prosperity, while the voters, after long years of 'unanimity', simply enjoyed choosing one candidate from among several and arguing about their virtues.

The disintegration of the old system of rule in turn provoked a crisis in the Communist Party leadership. The party bore responsibility for everything and had not yet come to terms with its role as the supreme co-ordinator of the system. The apparatchiks were showing a preference for comfortable posts with Soviet-Singaporean mixed enterprises, for speculating in computers, and for engaging in similar profitable ventures. The collapse of the old system of rule inevitably meant that party functionaries lost all hope of holding on to power, at any rate in the largest industrial centres. The transfer of power to the soviets, accompanied by the transfer of part of the nomenklatura from their armchairs as party apparatchiks to armchairs as deputies (whether they were designated as 'Communist' or liberal was unimportant) seemed to the hierarchy to be the best possible solution to a difficult problem.

The slogan of returning to the soviets the powers that had been taken from them did not come from below, and was not forced on the authorities by the popular movement. It was handed down from above in the speeches of Gorbachev and in official instructions to state officials. Naturally, the soviets involved were not those of 1917, which had long since ceased to exist, but the bureaucratized and powerless soviets bequeathed to us by Stalin, Khrushchev and Brezhnev. What emerged from this can readily be seen in the example of the Moscow Soviet.

In the city soviet elections in the spring of 1990 Muscovites elected a majority from the Democratic Russia bloc, which had called for a decisive transfer of power from party organs to popularly elected representatives. At the time, no one expected that the transition period would be easy. Everyone anticipated clashes between the new majority in the soviet on the one hand, and the Communist Party city committee and its supporters in the Moscow group of deputies on the other. Conflicts of this type did in fact arise. But they turned out to be far less dramatic than many deputies had expected.

Despite the fears of the democrats, the Moscow group did not obstruct the work of the soviet in a systematic or organized fashion. At the first session furious debates broke out on procedural questions, but on the whole the Moscow Soviet got down to work much more rapidly than did the Leningrad Soviet, whose democratic majority split into warring factions during the first days.

The real conflict was centred not on the question of power, but on that of responsibility. The Communist Party city leadership was happy to hand over responsibility for the neglected urban economy and for the political life of the capital, but on questions of party property, or what the Moscow party leaders considered to be their property, the party organs were ready to fight to the death. Everyone recalls how the newspaper *Vechernaya Moskva*, which had been founded by the soviet, and which had subsequently become a joint publication of the Moscow City Committee of the Communist Party and the Moscow Soviet, was unexpectedly transformed into party property. A prolonged dispute broke out over buildings which the previous executive committee had transferred to the account of the Communist Party. But all this constituted only an insignificant fraction of the party's property in the capital.

In essence, the Moscow City Committee of the Communist Party made up a large business empire which controlled finance capital, newspapers and real estate, and which resembled the empire of Donald Trump in New York, for example. When the Moscow Soviet gathered for its first session it was obliged to spend tens of thousands of rubles on hiring a hall in the House of Political Education belonging to the Communist Party. So the city soviet did not even have a hall big enough to accommodate all of the deputies and guests.

Representatives of the directorate of the Moscow City Committee complained that the rent was too low, barely covering the costs of maintaining the building. A great deal was said about how the Communist Party had no wish to monopolize the use of the House of Political Education and was ready to hand it over to other organizations. In the course of time it emerged that discussions were under way with an American firm on a project to turn the building into a joint venture leisure centre.

At the sessions of the Moscow Soviet's commission on social organizations the Socialist deputies argued that the building should be taken over by the municipality. But the liberal-minded majority refused to support this proposal; for them, private property was sacred.

The conflicts over *Vechernaya Moskva* and the House of Political Education were in fact the only disputes in which the Democratic Russia bloc and the Moscow bloc were ranged against one another. Contrary to expectations, the main clashes in the Moscow Soviet took place within the ranks of Democratic Russia. Here the interests of numerous fractions and groups came into collision, and struggles erupted between individual deputies. In most cases the groups taking part in such conflicts were not organized, did not have a political programme and arose and collapsed quite abruptly. From the outside this looked very like a war in which each individual was pitted against the rest.

The first days of the opening session were marked by an acute conflict between supporters of Popov and the followers of Stankevich. The 'division of labour' which accorded Stankevich an honourable second place on the presidium of the soviet did not quell the passions, since the question of the leadership of the commissions and the presidium was at stake, and it was precisely on this that the interest of the majority of deputies was concentrated. On the whole the behind-the-scenes struggle that accompanied the formation of the presidium differed little from the familiar battles within the nomenklatura in which each group sought to obtain its 'quota'. The greater the need to satisfy all and offend none, the more people were appointed to the presidium, and the faster the number of posts on the commissions increased.

The old model of forming the leadership was reproduced fully in the election for the post of president of the Executive Committee of the Moscow Soviet. In formal terms Gavriil Popov had to defeat several other candidates in order to be elected; Sergei Stankevich, Popov's only serious potential rival, was forced to withdraw his candidature before the election, in order, the public were told, 'to avoid splitting the democratic majority'. But in the elections for the second rank of the leadership there was generally no choice of candidate. Yuri Luzhkov's candidacy for the post of president of the Executive Committee went unopposed.

In essence, the soviet has turned out to be completely incapable not only of exercising real power, but even of demonstrating elementary control over its members and the structures which they set up. The presidium must be given its due; the heads of commissions and members of the presidium at least appear regularly at all the sessions. But those Muscovites who had the patience to sit through the second half of the first session of the Moscow Soviet probably recall the shameful moment when an adjournment had to take place for lack of a quorum, without the session having been concluded.

Condemn the deputies as one might, the problem is not confined to their 'low level of activity', about which the newspapers have done little to inform Moscow residents. The problem is that with its present structure and composition the soviet cannot be a viable organ of administration. Its 480 deputies, who furthermore are not organized into party fractions, are more like a crowd (or at best, a small political meeting) than an organ of political power. The logic which applies here is not that of political life but of mass consciousness. The deputies are readily swayed by emotion and are easily manipulated – always provided that these people can be assembled in the first place.

The way in which the soviet resolved to introduce trade 'by pass-ports' is more than suggestive. The deputies acted under the influence of their emotions, without having available to them either full informa-tion or competent expert analysis. Even in the difficult situation which had arisen in the city, such a question should not even have been discussed in the session unless experts had studied it beforehand. Several deputies, myself included, did not vote on the question, seeing no possibility of making a competent decision. Some voted against. The majority, swayed by their emotions, voted in favour. Next day Moscow found itself in a state of commercial war against all the neighbouring provinces, since funds for foodstuffs had originally been assigned to the capital on the presumption that the inhabitants of the neighbouring provinces would export the products which they did not require themselves. The Executive Committee of the Moscow Soviet published a long list of goods with details of the number which could be sold to each customer; this included men's underpants! And throughout the country soldiers began to be beaten up by their comrades from Moscow.

Afterwards many deputies voiced their objections, saying that the decision should not have been taken. But to put it more accurately, issues in general should not be decided in this fashion.

And when all is said and done, who runs the capital? Who exercises authority? The soviet is not the real power, and the city committee of the party has held itself aloof – taking, it seems, a certain pleasure in observing the soviet's difficulties. Real power is divided between the executive committee and the presidium of the soviet; at the head of this set-up are the president and his deputies. The presidium in turn rests on the commissions which prepare its resolutions. The question is: to what extent are all these structures able to act in concert?

The main problem with which the commissions are forced to con-tend is the lack of co-ordination between the various parts of the system and our own incompetence as deputies. Here again the blame lies not so much with the deputies or voters as with the structure which has arisen. Under the 'old regime' the city party leadership knew in advance who it needed to have on the commissions of the soviet. A certain number of architects, a certain number of economists and a certain number of lawyers had to be found. Specific people were chosen ahead of time. Whether this was good or bad is not so important; the main thing is that one way or another the system worked.

Naturally, when relatively free elections came along, the voters did not know or want to know about this. They did not know who was being elected in the neighbouring districts, and indeed this was not their business. Nor did they have any idea how many, let us say, architects the soviet would have in its ranks. The same thing happened in the regional soviets, with still more serious consequences. The Moscow Soviet was helped out to some extent by its 'mass character'; when you have five hundred deputies it is statistically probable that you will find one or two specialists in each area.

How are such problems solved in the West? In essence, in the same way as in the Soviet Union under the old regime, only on the basis of multi-party pluralism. Any serious party with aspirations to playing a dominant role in the organs of power knows that it must have specialists in various fields. The party selects its deputies in advance by placing its most capable people in the 'safest' districts, where their election is guaranteed. In the worst scenario, the parliamentary fractions seek the help of experts thoroughly versed in the questions at issue. Commissions are then formed in the same fashion, though with the participation of deputies chosen from various parties. The party or coalition that enjoys a majority controls the commissions, and through them pursues a single set of perspectives that is known in advance and is applied in a consistent fashion. In this way, competence is combined with co-ordinated action.

Everyone in the former Soviet Union is now rejoicing at the advent of multi-party pluralism, stressing that this is the basis for democracy. But they do not go on to explain what precisely the parties should be doing. There is more than enough work for the parties, but at present they are unable to carry it out, or have no wish to. Broad blocs of the Democratic Russia type, which are coalitions of informal groups and of independent high-placed politicians, are in principle unable to perform this work. They have neither a unified set of political perspectives, nor a single organizational apparatus, nor an ideological basis (if one ignores general phrases about the evils of totalitarianism and the benefits of democracy; these things are fine in opposition, but are inadequate for the exercise of power).

So it comes about that instead of dealing with the business of the city, we spend our time debating the question of whether or not to remove the bust of Lenin from the assembly hall. But at least we are all competent to make a decision on this issue.

If anything gets done, it is mainly due to the bureaucracy. We deplore this just as we used to, but without it the present soviet would simply collapse. The bureaucrats are all professionals of one kind or another. As a result of all this the bureaucracy has not only failed to shrink, but is apparently beginning to grow. Whatever the case, the bureaucratic structure is becoming more complex.

It turns out that we have several bureaucracies, in the good and bad senses of the word. The presidium and the commissions have their own apparatus, and so does the executive committee. In 1990 the budget of the soviet, which is independent of the budget of the executive committee and of general city spending, amounted to about 5 million rubles, not really such a large sum though an astronomical one considering how meagre were the results of our work over the year.

In the final analysis all questions are decided within the triangle of the commissions, the presidium and the executive committee. Here the scope for bureaucratic games is boundless. The role played by the sessions of the soviet is becoming steadily less important, particularly since obtaining a quorum is growing more and more difficult. The deputies in turn are confronted with the question: what should their priorities be – policy matters in the commissions or the affairs of their districts? In a system based on political parties responsibility for this or that matter can be handed over to fellow deputies in the party fractions, ensuring a co-ordinated division of labour (this is what the Socialist Party fraction in the Moscow Soviet tried to do). But independent deputies must be everything at once and must take independent decisions on all questions. They are both politicians and administrative 'fixers' for their constituents. Combining these functions is becoming increasingly difficult, and as a result the deputies are coming more and more to be divided into two groups that have little in common.

Initially, attempts to hold open discussions on the need to reform the soviet were met 'with fixed bayonets' by the leadership and by the majority of deputies who supported it. 'To criticize the new soviets means playing into the hands of the party regime.' 'Anyone who criticizes Democratic Russia puts wind into the sails of the Communist Party.' 'Anyone who is not with us is against us.' These were the responses whenever anyone took issue with supporters of the new leadership. But even the Democratic Russia deputies very soon began to recognize that the city administration needed radical reform, and that the 'renewed' organs of power were transitional in nature and, by virtue of this, had already ceased to be workable. The sooner they disappear from the scene the better.

As early as the spring of 1990 the Socialist deputy Vladimir Kondratov put forward suggestions for such a reform. In his view the weaknesses of the Moscow Soviet could be overcome if the whole system were drastically simplified. Instead of more than thirty small regional soviets, he said, we need nine or ten zonal municipalities with real powers and responsibilities. On the neighbourhood level power should be transferred to the soviets of the microregions. The number of deputies to the city soviet should be much smaller, a maximum of 100 to 150. There should be a single executive body, since the existence of both the executive committee and the presidium represents an absurd duplication of powers, an outlandish bureaucratic caprice.

Within six months the idea of administrative reform had also begun to take hold in the minds of the new city bureaucracy. A proposal for transforming the city administration began circulating in the Moscow Soviet. But this idea as interpreted by the city leadership proved rather different from its form in the mouths of radical deputies. The regional soviets, which until this time had basically succeeded only in quarrelling with the city authorities, were abolished, and their powers were transferred in part to the microregions. Together with the abolition of the old structure of the soviets, democratic structures in general were then abolished on the city level.

The Socialists considered it essential for the success of the municipal reform that new soviets should be created on the basis of real multiparty pluralism. Only in this way would electors get the chance not just to vote for good people, but to choose between alternative party programmes, between the different conceptions of development for the city or urban district. However, the reform that was implemented had the effect of consolidating the personal power of the president of the presidium, Gavriil Popov. The new administrators found they could get along fine without soviets. The elections helped the leadership create its bureaucratic structures of power, and from that point any further playing at democracy became superfluous. In place of municipalities or soviets of a new type there appeared administrative organs subordinated to the central power, with the ruler of Moscow personally accountable only to the ruler of Russia, Boris Yeltsin, and with the rulers of the regions accountable to the ruler of the city. In this way the authorities once again became fully independent of the population.

On 16 September the supporters of Democratic Russia, which had long since ceased to be a united political bloc, came out on to the streets of Moscow in response to the summons of Gavriil Popov and his associates. Muscovites had grown accustomed to demonstrations, but this time, along with the demands for the resignation of the Soviet government and for the implementation of 'radical reform', entirely new elements appeared. One example was the demand for 'Order in the city!' The city authorities were hinting at intrigues by some dark force or other that was supposed to be responsible for the collapse of the urban economy and for all the rest of the city's troubles. Of course, it was clear to anyone who was really familiar with the work of the Moscow Soviet that the main source of the problems was the new city administration, which was unable or unwilling to provide for the needs of the population.

The following example illustrates the attitude which the rulers of Moscow held towards its citizens. During one of the television interviews which are so beloved of the new leaders, Gavriil Popov was asked a question about refugees. The president of the Moscow Soviet replied: 'In Moscow there are twenty thousand refugees, and a few dozen deputies are addressing their problems. Meanwhile there are several hundred thousand dogs, and no one is bothering about them.'[1] The ruler of the capital refused to reply to the numerous protests which this remark provoked, while his close associate Mikhail Schneider – until recently a Socialist and a comrade of mine in the Moscow Popular Front – explained that several minutes before the interview a note about the pitiful condition of the city's dogs had landed on the desk of the president of the Moscow Soviet. 'This note', Schneider continued, 'made such a strong impression on Gavriil Kharitonovich, who is a great lover of animals, that in answering the television viewer's question about refugees, he involuntarily linked these two problems.'[2] Further comment would be superfluous. . . .

Overall, it appears that only one question has seriously preoccupied the capital's leaders. As Popov put it, Moscow and the country as a whole have many problems, 'but the main thing is still this: state property has to be dismantled'. Yuri Luzhkov spoke much more specifically:

> In the next five years the level of privatization in everyday services must reach a level of 70 to 75 per cent, and in trade 50 per cent, while the remaining half of the enterprises in the trading sector must be in the form of joint stock companies. In the production of consumer goods the level of privatization must be 60 per cent, and in foodstuffs 15–20 per cent, with the remainder joint stock firms in which the share of state capital can still be relatively large. Urban catering services must be completely private.[4]

In reality the aim is complete privatization, since in practice there is no difference between joint stock and individual private property. The role played by the state in the economy, the Moscow leaders contend, should be reduced to speculating in shares in the stock exchange or supporting uncompetitive enterprises so that private shareholders who have put money into them will not risk losing it.

Absorbed in passionate debate on how to redistribute property, the liberal and populist politicians have given virtually no thought to the question of how to escape from the economic crisis. It is as though transferring state property into private hands were enough to change everything; as though, once this was done, economic relations would put themselves right, inflation would disappear, the threat of unemployment would vanish, wages would begin to rise, and old equipment would be replaced by new without additional capital investments.

In this instance both the liberal politicians and their supporters 'among the public' have reasoned along the same lines as the participants in collectivization: the main thing is to take property away from its present owners, and then all the problems will solve themselves. The only difference is that the participants in collectivization by and large believed that they were taking property away from the 'kulaks' in order to give it to 'everyone', while the new capitalist reformers have known from the beginning that the property will belong to a chosen few.

In both cases the slogan of the redivision of property was easily taken up by the lumpenized crowd. And in both cases the lumpenized mass would receive nothing or almost nothing from this great redistribution; whether property was 'collectivized' or 'privatized', it would not come into the possession of the people in the street. In both cases the impassioned outbursts and calls for redistribution for the sake of redistribution were only a cover for behind-the-scenes manipulation and for preparing favourable conditions for dictatorship.

Towards the end of 1990 the rulers of Soviet society at all levels were calling in chorus for emergency powers. Several months previously when the post of president had been created and the constitution amended to give Gorbachev enormous powers, there were still people who asked: 'Were the rights he enjoyed as supreme leader of the USSR, as president of the Supreme Soviet and General Secretary of the Communist Party, really not enough for him?' But by autumn Gorbachev was declaring that these powers were too limited and that he needed greater authority. The rulers at lower levels, in the republics, the cities and even the urban regions, said the same. All of them complained of powerlessness and demanded new rights. This was accompanied by perorations on the law-governed state and the authority of law; no one troubled to recall that initially these concepts had been advanced not in order to justify broadening the powers of the executive authority, but to protect the rights of citizens.

Meanwhile the position of Moscow residents had worsened dramatically. The shops were bare, cigarettes had vanished, and so for a time had bread. By September it was already clear that there would be problems in providing heating to residential districts. The city leaders sought to heap the blame for this chaos on 'sabotage' by the old bureaucrats and the central government, refusing to accept any responsibility for it themselves. In a country used to centralized government, people believed this out of habit. Meanwhile, Popov and his circle insisted that they be given unlimited power.

The democratic experiment in the city had obviously failed. Despite the misgivings of the public, its gravediggers were not the old bureaucrats and Communists, but a new oligarchy that had arisen under the slogan of the struggle for democracy and renewal. But was anything really new? Most of the leaders of Democratic Russia had their origins in the old apparatus, and had represented particular groupings within it. The formation of a solid bloc of Communists and liberals was going ahead at full speed. Meanwhile, Muscovites stood in queues, bought cigarettes at prices that made smoking a luxury for the elite, and awaited miracles from the promised government programme for a transition to capitalism within five hundred days.

Notes

1. *Kommersant*, no. 28, 1990, p. 15.
2. Ibid.
3. *Kuranty*, no. 1, 1990, p. 4.
4. *Kommersant*, no. 28, 1990, p. 3.

5

Pluralism Russian Style: A Multiplicity of Good Parties?

The official proclamation of multi-party pluralism in 1990 created a mass of attractive possibilities for professional and semi-professional politicians, but left the average citizen in some bewilderment. Dozens of confusing names and abbreviations have flashed across the newspapers. In most cases these are micro-parties, rival grouplets which zealously accuse one another of having insignificant memberships. But how can serious mass organizations emerge in a vacuum? And how is the newspaper reader, receiving extremely scanty and often unreliable information, to understand which of these groups have the potential to become significant political forces? Striving by any means possible to prove their seriousness, the organizers of the new parties try to get publicity by recruiting celebrities – just as if they were trying to sell new wares in the marketplace.

However, the main problem for the organizers of parties is different. The majority of organizations are, as it were, cut from the same cloth, and it is practically impossible to distinguish one from another not only on the basis of their programmes and slogans, but also of their tactics. When one of the activists of the Liberal-Democratic Party was asked to outline the party's programme he replied proudly: 'It's just like all the others! Multiple forms of property, parliamentary democracy and a free market!'

In fact, these three slogans summed up the political wisdom of the country, since in this regard the Communist leaders did not differ from the most rabid liberals. A comparison of the programmatic declarations of Bryachikhin, who was nominated for the post of president of the Moscow Soviet by deputies standing 'on the platform of the City Committee of the Communist Party of the Soviet Union', and those of Gavriil Popov, the representative of the Democratic Russia bloc, showed striking unity on all the key points. True, there were many who still did not believe that the Communists had become defenders of

77

private property. But the evidence was there. The CPSU of 1990–91 had become the largest commercial organization in the country, and made profitable use of its assets – newspapers, buildings rented out for public meetings and so forth. If even the liberals of the Moscow Soviet were forced to pay tens of thousands of rubles to the City Committee of the Communist Party for the hire of a hall in which to hold their sessions, then it had to be recognized that Soviet Communists had business sense.

In these circumstances the opposition parties differed from the businessmen of the CPSU not in their programme, but in their greater or lesser flair for advertising themselves with the help of anti-communist rhetoric. This was and remains especially typical of former Communists. Anti-communism was proclaimed as the basic ideological doctrine of the Democratic Party of Russia, founded by Nikolai Travkin (the original name of this organization was the People's Party). Most of its founders, including its leader, came from the Democratic Platform group in the CPSU. Attempting to broaden his social base, Travkin tried to unite in his party the organizing committees of a number of other bodies – of the co-operators' Party of Free Labour, of one of the peasant parties then in the process of formation, and also the leaders of the armed forces union Shield, of the writers' committee April, and of the Russian Popular Front (not to be confused with the Moscow Popular Front, which the leaders of the Russian Popular Front regarded with open hostility because of its sizeable Jewish and socialist membership).

It stands to reason that Travkin's success in uniting the leaders of these organizations within his party did not mean that all their members and supporters gave the Democratic Party their unconditional loyalty. But for the ideologists of the party this was enough to declare their organization 'the party for all the people', like the CPSU in its time. The simplicity of its slogans and the familiar ring of its ideological language, together with the presence of large numbers of the traditional elite, made the Democratic Party a favourite with the official mass media.

The leaders of this party could not boast of a prolonged record of struggle against totalitarianism, but made up for this lack by issuing furiously anti-communist statements. Like most other parties, they gave pride of place to the demand for the introduction of a free market and private entrepreneurship as a recipe for saving the country. In an interview with *Literaturnaya Gazeta* Travkin let it be clearly understood that in this regard he was ready to go even further than Reagan, since the crisis in the USSR was deeper. Travkin's followers rejected not only the CPSU, but also social democracy, insisting that their party, with its significant proportion of former Communists, had nothing in common with socialism (and this, of course, is something one could not possibly dispute). What they were proposing was one of the variants of 'shock therapy', and they were forming a party which in the West would be described as right-wing conservative. The signs are that many of the most conservative American senators could work within this party without being suspected of closet sympathies with Communists.

The anti-communist slogans of Travkin and his followers mainly attracted people from the 'common crowd', including a certain number of skilled workers – the very people whom capitalism, in all likelihood, would not just put out of work, but would put out into the street. As always, the declassed masses were being invited to pull the chestnuts out of the fire for a new set of masters, who promised them prosperity once the guilty had been punished and property had been redistributed.

Of course, Travkin and his followers, or for that matter the Free Democrats who split off from them, are not the only variety of right-wingers in Russia.[1] The liberals present a whole spectrum of formations and organizations, the largest of which are the Union of Constitutional Democrats and the Liberal-Democratic Party. These groups have not yet succeeded in establishing where the difference between their pro-grammes lies, but substantial differences nonetheless exist. The Constitutional Democrats had their origins in the informal movements, and were formerly participants either in the youth group Civil Dignity or in the Democratic Fraction of the Moscow Popular Front, which split from the Socialist majority in the spring of 1989. The Liberal Democrats, on the other hand, emerged as an organized current only in the spring of 1990, when political pluralism was officially proclaimed. Its leader, Zhirinovsky, soon began to make a name for himself with demagogic nationalist appeals.

We also have Social Democrats. The founding congress of the Social Democratic Party of the Russian Federation took place on 4 May 1989. Earlier, the Social Democratic Association had been formed; along with the groups which made up the Social Democratic Party, this included others which for various reasons stayed out. The leader of both organizations is Oleg Rumyantsev, who in the spring of 1990 was elected a People's Deputy of the Russian Republic.

At a certain stage the ideas of social democracy enjoyed tremendous popularity in the country, though this was later to evaporate. Social democracy was associated in the public consciousness with a humane and democratic capitalism in which the shelves of shops are full, private enterprise flourishes, health care and education are free, and there is no unemployment. In short, the wolves have full bellies and the sheep are all intact. The difficulty lay in explaining how these miracles were to come about under Soviet conditions. The precondition for the success of social democracy in the West is the existence of an efficient capitalism whose products can be redistributed. But how can this be if there is no capitalism? Capitalism has to be created, say the Social Democrats. Speaking on television, the party's ideologue, the economist Saltan Dzarasov, acknowledged only two principles: private property and private enterprise. There were in fact no clear differences between Social Democrats and right-wing liberals; some journalists in the unofficial press pointed out that this was yet another liberal party. In this respect the Social Democrats differed markedly from those in the West, who attempt to restrain the market and to place certain restrictions on private enterprise.

In the autumn of 1990 the Social Democrats formed a 'united bloc' with Travkin's Democratic Party and with the Democratic Platform party, consisting of former Communists who had embraced liberal positions. In essence this meant a single right-liberal bloc.

So Where Was the Left?

It is clear that by no means all the participants in Soviet political life were euphoric over the accelerated introduction of capitalism. If private property and the free market – in the West, the central tenets of the ideology of the right – are the latest ideological fashion in our country, it is inevitable that an opposition to these concepts will also arise, orienting itself to the traditional values and principles of the left: solidarity, social responsibility, collective forms of property, self-management and so on. But to establish such an opposition after decades of a totalitarian Communist regime is an extremely difficult matter, especially under the present conditions of ideological confusion.

The orthodox Communists were trying to unite within the framework of the Russian Communist Party; feeling that the businessmen in the capital had betrayed them, lecturers in Marxism-Leninism and middle-level functionaries flocked beneath its banners. By the autumn of 1990 there was also a significant democratic socialist opposition within the ranks of the CPSU and the Russian Communist Party. This was composed primarily of a section of the activists of the Marxist Platform tendency, grouped around Alexander Buzgalin. But naturally, these people did not determine the ideological face of the two parties as a whole. To the degree that the supporters of democratic socialism in the ranks of the official party had recognized the impossibility of ever turning the CPSU into a genuinely democratic organization, they drew closer to the Socialists.

The extreme left was represented by two micro-parties, the Democratic Workers Party (Marxist) and the Marxist Workers Party/Party of the Dictatorship of the Proletariat; these achieved a degree of notoriety in the press. Despite their small size these groups had a certain number of supporters in the workers' movement. The supporters of the MWP-PDP rejected parliamentarism and the market economy, which at least gave them a distinctive place on the current political scene, but they did not advance any serious alternative socio-economic programme. The DWP(M) at first displayed a more moderate approach and a certain pluralism of viewpoints, but has since inclined to the traditional Bolshevik model of the party. A split occurred in the MWP in the autumn of 1990 and a group of its former members united with a section of the DWP(M) to establish a new Bolshevik-style party. Those who remained in the MWP preferred to mention the dictatorship of the proletariat as little as possible.

In formal terms the Confederation of Anarcho-Syndicalists (CAS) would have to be included as part of the left. Although its leaders did not acknowledge it as a party, the CAS participated in elections, admittedly without much success, and had its own organs of propaganda. It was the first of the new political groups to be officially proclaimed. The group's central ideological concepts – agitation for self-management and for the holding of property by workers' collectives – were not, however, reflected in an independent tactical line. The CAS generally acted as the junior partner of the liberal groups, postponing the clarification of its relations with them until more propitious times. To judge from the anarcho-syndicalist press, the CAS regarded its main enemies as being other leftists who did not share its ideology.

The Socialists represented a case apart. The Socialists rejected utopian thinking based on worship of the plan or idealization of the market. In their view attempts to implant Western economic models in Russian soil could only lead to an exacerbation of the crisis and to new violence against society. The country lacks, and may always lack, the main precondition for the capitalist or social-democratic road: a competent and socially responsible bourgeoisie, of the kind which took centuries to develop in the West. We do not have a Protestant ethic, without which it is difficult to imagine civilized entrepreneurship. For this reason it is impossible to envisage the successful development of the ex-Soviet Union along the social-democratic path.

As an alternative to Russia's transformation into a Third World country the Socialists proposed the establishment of an efficient and democratically organized state sector. People today are attempting to limit the role of the state in the economy not because they seriously believe in private enterprise, but because everyone detests the old totalitarianism. The task, however, was to create a new, democratic state based on the participation of the masses in the process of administration. The Socialists called for combining the plan and market on the basis of democratic decision-making, for transferring state property to the soviets at various levels and for handing over a significant portion of enterprises to the ownership of self-governing workers' collectives. They did not object to the existence of privately owned enterprises. The private sector must develop through the construction of new enterprises, not through speculation or though buying up shares in the state sector. The creation of new jobs and of socially necessary products in the private sector could be guaranteed only through the dynamic growth of the socialized economy and through effective decentralized planning.

The Socialist Party, whose founding conference was held in the summer of 1990, often came into conflict with a united front of opponents, from Russian nationalists to social democrats and from liberals to Communists. The Marxist terminology used by the Socialists had been compromised by official propaganda. One of the leaders of the opposition in the Komsomol, Alexander Bek, once observed that the new Socialists articulate popular ideas in an idiom which is extremely unpopular. But for the party to employ a different language or to try to adapt itself to fashionable moods would be still more damaging. The Socialist Party set out to popularize its ideas through its actions, in strike committees and organs of local self-government. Instead of marching in step, as the rules of totalitarian society dictate, the Socialists were trying to follow their own path, if necessary against the prevailing ideological current.

Many Dangers – But Which of Them Are Real?

People were scared of many things. Some argued about the inevitability of civil war, others talked of a military coup, while still others expected pogroms against Jews. Rumours about Anti-Semitic pogroms by the organization Pamyat started flying on average twice a year, after which reports of impending attacks on Jews appear in the Western press, calling forth panic on both sides of the Atlantic and forcing American legislators to discuss the question of restoring political refugee status for ex-Soviet citizens seeking an economic haven in the developed capitalist world.

No one doubted that political chaos lay ahead. The more chaos people see in prospect, the more inclined they are to demand a strong regime and a 'firm hand'. A 'general president' with dictatorial powers was proposed, a concept which, in the words of the deputy Vladimir Kondratov, differed little from the absolutism of the Emperor and Autocrat of All the Russias. This was no longer Communist totalitarianism. And it was not yet, or had ceased to be, democracy. The ruler issues a decree setting out his new powers. These powers are not all that much greater than before, and the powers of the General Secretary used to be just as boundless. But the institution of the presidency was designed for different conditions and had other purposes.

In place of the power of the party we had the power of a political elite, resting on laws which it drafted itself in order to serve its own goals. If the Communist Party elite had become super-property-owners, and if the profit from party newspapers had become more important than the ideology they presented, then the state must not propagate any ideology, but must defend the rights of the property-owners from any incursions by the dispossessed. Power was becoming more and more deideologized but no less authoritarian – even more so by comparison with the last two years. Social instability, a climate of fear and the struggle of individuals against one another have definite advantages where this power is concerned. Let the Armenians go to war with the Azerbaijanis, let the poor hate the rich, and let everyone compete among themselves in the hope of seizing at least some part of the former social pie. For the authorities, this was not a danger but a vindication. What they found dangerous was social solidarity and the self-organization of social forces.

The stability of power was guaranteed by the atomization and dog-eat-dog struggle of private interests. In Russia at the end of the twentieth century the principle of divide and rule was acquiring a new meaning: divide up state property in order to retain the old anti-popular state and the old power.

The 'Petrakov Plan'

In the spring of 1990 observers in the West were discussing the 'Petrakov Plan', named in honour of Gorbachev's new adviser. Our own commentators began to write about a 'leap into the market', a 'new radical reform' and so forth. What lay behind these concepts?

After proclaiming the principle of the plan-market economy, our leaders presented the country with the next slogan in the same series, decreeing that 'the economy must be economic'. Every modern economy includes elements of planning and elements of the market. An unplanned market is something out of the eighteenth century. A plan without a market is something which also belongs strictly to the realm of propaganda; so long as money, wage payments and commodities exist, the more or less developed elements of a market will exist as well. True, opinion differed as to the existence of commodities in our society, and as to the manner of finding them. . . . But this is a purely practical question.

The real problem was not in proclaiming the existence of the market, but in understanding which market structures it was necessary to introduce, how to introduce them and, most importantly of all, why. Answering these questions was impossible until another question had been answered: who was all this meant to benefit?

Our society is still dominated by an ideological habit of thought, a conviction on the part of a significant number of our fellow citizens, according to which all our problems would be solved if we could just proclaim the correct slogan and stand firmly behind it. If the words 'market', 'capital', 'private property' and 'free enterprise' have been banned for many years, then is this not the cause of all our troubles? We must shout these slogans louder, and go forward!

The East European Laboratory

The reform policies conceived in the USSR in 1985 intensified the crisis of the system in the countries of Eastern and Central Europe that along with us had formed the 'socialist camp'. The near-universal collapse of the 'Communist' regimes of the region in the autumn and winter of 1989 created a qualitatively new situation when in their implementation of liberal reforms, these countries not only overtook the Soviet Union in a matter of days, but far outstripped it. Most of the East European countries were ahead of the Soviet Union in their level of industrial development, and had much stronger traditions of democratic and bourgeois development. It would seem, therefore, that in these countries conditions would be much more propitious for the success of a liberal experiment.

In the course of 1989 and 1990 the territory of the former satellite countries of the Stalinist empire was transformed into a huge polygon in which the ideas and theories of the new liberal capitalism were being tried out. Especially important in this respect were the events in Poland and Hungary, where the collapse of the 'old regime' and the formation of new ruling groups began significantly earlier than in the other 'fraternal countries'. The experiences in Poland and Hungary are the main source of inspiration for reformers in the Soviet Union throughout the 1980s (this applies in equal degree both to the official and to the opposition circles).

If anyone could have illusions concerning the politics of the 'general good', then the experience of Poland and Hungary had shown graphically that behind the slogans of the transition to the market there was a project aimed at securing the interests of definite social strata. These policies were formulated most consistently in the well-known 'Balcerowicz Plan', christened in honour of the finance minister in Mazowiecki's government. In line with the recommendations of the International Monetary Fund, subsidies on foodstuffs and other goods were abolished, state controls on prices were ended, and shares in state enterprises began to be sold off to private buyers, including foreign ones. Simultaneously, wages were frozen. In the view of the plan's authors, this last element was critical for its success.

The removal of subsidies and the ending of the price freeze led, naturally enough, to rapid inflation. And since wages were frozen, the demand for goods declined sharply. It was not only luxuries that people ceased to buy; often, they began to deny themselves the very necessities of life. The fall in demand led to a curtailment of production; enterprises began to shut down, unemployment appeared, and the economy plunged into depression. Meanwhile, the plan's authors pronounced it a success. First of all, inflation had ceased, which was especially important for people with significant savings. Second, the possibility had emerged of buying up, at cut rates, a significant part of the state's capital assets.

Predictably, the new owners were mainly people who had occupied privileged positions under the old regime. This aroused widespread discontent among the population, but the nomenklatura found numerous defenders among the 'democrats'. Jacek Kuron, who not long before had been a social democrat, argued on becoming labour minister in Mazowiecki's government that the circumstances resulting from the plan would make it easier for the former ruling circles to part with power.

The Soviet commentator Eduard Gonzalez argued in *Izvestiya* that there was nothing alarming about the seizure of state property by the bureaucracy throughout Eastern Europe. People were complaining about the seizure of property by the mafia and corrupt bureaucrats, he wrote, only because they feared that they themselves would get nothing. Meanwhile, he stated, the process was creating a group of citizens who not only collectively but also individually were vitally interested in the market. 'Out of this group,' he wrote, 'will emerge the merchants and entrepreneurs; there is simply nowhere else they will be found. The fact that such a manner of preparing the subjects of market relations will hardly prove pleasing to others is a quite different issue.'[2]

In reality, sad to say, everything has turned out quite differently. The problem is not only the identity of the owners, but also the structure of property arising in the country, the type of market which is being formed, and the type of links which are being established between the people whom Gonzalez refers to graciously as the 'subjects of market relations'. The structure which is being created reproduces the very worst features of the 'old order'.

In essence, what had occurred was a 'conversion' of power into property. The old system of links and relationships underwent a radical reconstruction, but on the whole survived and was even strengthened. Small independent entrepreneurs (the analogues of our co-operators) gained little, since the cost to them of lost production as a result of lowered living standards and economic depression was heavy. The masses of hired workers lost out. Still suffering from exploitation, they have lost their former social guarantees. In Poland, according to the calculations of Western journalists, the 60 or so per cent of the population who are dependent on wages have been forced to reconcile themselves to a 40 per cent fall in their living standards. About 20 per cent of Poles have maintained their living standards, and the top 20 per cent have improved their position, often in striking fashion.

The middle strata, who had hoped for a rapid improvement in their lives under capitalism, also felt the acuteness of the crisis. A Polish journalist wrote in a liberal Soviet publication:

When at the beginning of the year we began the 'shock leap into the market economy', we did not fully appreciate the scale of the sacrifices which this difficult surgical operation would demand of us. Now everyone understands this in a highly personal way. Purchases of foodstuffs have fallen by almost 40 per cent. The structure of consumption has changed sharply. We have had to give up many services we used to avail ourselves of as a matter of course. Most of us did not manage to take a winter break in the mountains, though this was easier to bear since the weather this year let us down. Children spent the winter vacation at home. Generally speaking we have given up outings to the cinema or the theatre, satisfying ourselves with television. Many people have been forced to give up books and newspapers, which have been much more interesting since the abolition of censorship. The restaurants and cafés are empty. The taxis stand in long, sad lines at the ranks. Purchases of cosmetics, clothes and even medicines have fallen off.[3]

Those experiencing the deprivation referred to here are the intelligentsia, representatives of 'decent society'. Much of what the journalist consumed 'as a matter of course' had already become inaccessible to workers and individual peasant farmers. These strata are feeling the crisis much more keenly. But in the final analysis this is not the main point. People can survive a few bad years if there is a 'shining future' ahead. But there is no light visible at the end of the tunnel, and the 'gleaming heights' of capitalism are turning out to be just as illusory as the communist paradise.

The struggle against inflation, considered the main priority of Mazowiecki's government, did not have the expected results. Although inflation rates dropped initially, by the end of 1990 official figures put inflation at 558 per cent. The wage freeze, presented by the new regime's ideologues as a temporary measure to help in the struggle against inflation, led only to a cut in living standards, not to an improvement in state finances.

The dissatisfaction of the East European people with the policies of the new regimes has naturally begun to increase. If initially people had confidence in the governments which saved them from the Communists and from Soviet control, then it very quickly emerged that the power of Moscow had been exchanged for the rule of the International Monetary Fund, while the promised economic revival was failing to eventuate. The popularity of the government in Poland and other East European countries began to fall as the first strikes were called and the first clashes took place between workers and the authorities. The government's supporters began to call for the use of repression against the strikers, who were undermining the economic programme which the new regime had negotiated with the Western creditors. The American journalist Joan Landy wrote:

> Supporters of democracy in the West must ask themselves the question: are the economic policies now being pursued in Eastern Europe by the US and other Western countries undermining the enormous democratic gains of 1989? Ultimately, the European Community, the US Congress, the International Monetary Fund, the World Bank and other Western institutions have declared unequivocally that the lightening of the debt burden and economic help to the post-Communist regimes depend on their quickly constructing market-capitalist economies. But thanks to the construction of such economies the Eastern European governments are having to sack millions of

workers, lower wages, and cut subsidies on foodstuffs, transport and other necessities.[4]

What effects would such methods have in Russia? Above all a dramatic strengthening of the position of the bureaucratic elite, which was vitally interested in transforming the ministries and departments, now powerless and of use to no one, into monopolistic concerns. The apparatus was being 'bourgeoisified', but in no way had it acquired the 'entrepreneurial spirit'. On the basis of the renewal of the old oligarchy a 'bureaucratic capital' was arising. This new formation was hostile in principle to the workers and blocked the development of entrepreneurial activity 'from below'. With Russia's level of development and inherited institutions, such a road would not lead to the promised leap into prosperity, or to catching up with the West. Instead, it would be a road to Third World status, Our choice would not be between Sweden and America, but between India and Bangladesh.[5]

The Computer and the Spade

The hoodwinked consumer, who first had been promised 'the construction of communism' – that is, an abundance of goods 'better than in America' by 1980 – and was then forced to buy sugar with ration coupons, did not want to stand in queues and hoped that the free market would solve all problems, 'as in the West'. Unfortunately the crisis to which we had fallen victim did not simply consist of shortages of foodstuffs and empty shelves in shops, though naturally this was the aspect of it which hit consumers hardest.

What we were confronting was actually a many-sided structural crisis. The economies of Eastern Europe and the Soviet Union were isolated for decades from the outside world, but continued developing in parallel, installing new technology and ensuring the growth of production and living standards. But by the end of the 1980s the economic structure which had arisen was no longer adequate for these tasks. And at the same time it was clearly not integrated into the international division of labour.

A number of interrelated problems emerged simultaneously:

1. The technological backwardness of all the former Communist countries compared with the countries of the West meant that the more closely the East becomes integrated in the international division of

labour, the more dependent it becomes, and this dooms us to the persistence of low living standards, to the transfer on to our territory from the 'advanced' countries of obsolete and environmentally destructive production, and so forth.

2. Outmoded economic structures, established for the most part in the 1940s and 1950s, cannot offer a solution to the problems of the 1990s. In addition, these economic structures are fundamentally anti-environmental.

3. The inadequate development of roads, transport and modern means of communication in Russia excluded any possibility of rapid modernization and made forming the structures of a contemporary economy impossible. Even the possibility of developed market relations was excluded.

4. The inadequacy of health care and education compared to social needs was becoming especially tragic in a changed world where the renewal of production and the material well-being of workers depended more and more on their qualifications, knowledge, culture and ability continually to re-educate themselves.

In the West all these tasks were resolved, more or less successfully, in the period from the 1930s to the 1960s. It should be noted that they were not solved by market methods. The decisive role in this period was played by state regulation, including direct capital investment by the state. The nationalized sector of the economy expanded.

It is clear that the present-day Western economies are far from ideal. But there are certain preconditions for modernization which any country must ensure if it wants to become a full-blooded part of the modern world. It is certainly not obligatory to imitate the West in increasing the number of cars, in practising wasteful consumption, or in destroying the environment. But whatever option we choose, we cannot do without a developed network of roads, a reliable telephone service, or universities where people can acquire useful knowledge. It was precisely the success of modernization in the West after the Second World War that allowed the economies of the leading capitalist countries to raise themselves to a qualitatively new level. This subsequently made a further development in the market possible. When the state structures had performed their function in the process of modernization, the bourgeoisie no longer needed them, and the corporations saw the democratic state not as an asset but as an obstacle, a bureaucracy tying them down. Neoconservative politicians in the West were much more successful than social democrats in understanding this new reality and in securing the changes the capitalist economies required. But what does this neoconservative Western model mean for the former Eastern bloc and the Third World?

It is typical that what the International Monetary Fund and the other capitalist organizations demand of the countries of Eastern Europe and the Third World is the exact opposite of what the Western countries themselves did in similar circumstances. It is quite clear that centralized totalitarian planning has shown itself to be completely incapable of carrying out the new tasks. After beginning to modernize the country, the bureaucratic regime proved incapable of completing the process. In the final analysis, this was why it collapsed. But the liquidation of the state sector and the abolition of the mechanisms of planning will not in themselves bring us any closer to success.

Even in East Germany, the most developed country of the former Communist bloc, integration into the world capitalist market has brought about a wave of bankruptcies, while many enterprises generally recognized as being technologically advanced are experiencing difficulties. 'In a diseased forest you even have to chop down healthy trees, if a healthy forest is ever to grow,'[6] a representative of the West German concern Siemens reasoned philosophically when asked about the future of the East German electronics industry. This recalls the well-known saying of Stalinist times, 'When you chop down a forest, chips are going to fly.' The trouble is that in both cases what is involved is not trees or chips, but the fate of millions of human beings.

Many people place their hopes on an infusion of Western capital. Since we do not have our own entrepreneur class, and the new owners are unwilling and unable to invest funds in modernizing the economy, all that was left was to sell ourselves into servitude. 'However objectionable they may find the role of apprentice, Soviet entrepreneurs who are establishing joint ventures with foreign firms must obviously reconcile themselves to it,' argued an expert in a right wing-liberal Moscow journal. 'How can we be of interest to experienced Western producers except as a source of cheap labour? The overwhelming majority of joint ventures operate on the principle of subordination, of master and apprentice, not of equal partnership.'[7]

Alas, here as well disappointment awaited us. The cheap labour force of Russia and Eastern Europe was a myth. The low wages in the countries of the former 'Communist camp' are compensated by state subsidies on housing, transport, foodstuffs and so on. In other words, the state subsidizes not only low-priced meat and milk, but also the price of labour power. So long as the state remained the only employer, this made sense. The sums invested in 'programmes of social development' returned to the budget via the profits of state enterprises. But with the privatization of property things are changing completely. The state now has no interest in subsidizing private profits, and anyway lacks the funds for such beneficence.

Maintaining 'social programmes' in conditions of privatization is possible only through high taxes, 'as in Sweden'. But we are not in Sweden. As we know, high taxes do not stimulate entrepreneurial activity. Since we cannot attract capital either by having a high level of development or through political stability, it is clear that the 'Swedish model' is of no use to us.

If we take account not only of the funds spent by the state on social programmes and on maintaining low food prices, but also of the general level of development of the economy, then it becomes clear that by international standards labour power in the East European countries is impossibly expensive!

The transition to the market means one of two things: after the abolition of subsidies the present living standards of the population will either be maintained as the price to the purchaser of labour power rises steeply, or living standards will fall sharply as previous wage levels are retained.

As the experience of Eastern Europe in 1990–91 showed, what happens in practice is something in between: living standards fall, but not so rapidly as to prevent a rise in the price of labour power. This makes our economies extremely uncompetitive on the world market and unattractive to international capital. There are two possible solutions:

1. Living standards can be lowered to the point where labour power really is cheap, or, more precisely, where the cost of labour power corresponds to the general low level of economic development.

2. The economy can be 'fired up', the level of development quickly raised, and expensive labour power made economically effective.

The second solution demands not only significant capital investments, a programme of technological renovation and so forth, but also a political regime which serves not the interests of capital but the interests of the workers. It must be clearly recognized that within the framework of the 'capitalist road' only the first solution is possible.

The collapse of the market experiment in Russia and Eastern Europe will be catastrophic only for the inhabitants of these regions. The Western transnational corporations will have little difficulty in extracting profits from these countries even if the position of their populations grows steadily worse.

Meanwhile, for the most advanced sector of production in the former Eastern bloc and for the qualified sectors of its workforce the question is a quite different one: to be or not to be?

There is a liberal myth that in a free market the most skilled worker and the entrepreneur using the most modern technology automatically win out. However, this rule applies only to highly developed countries with expensive labour power and 'cheap' technology, and even then there are significant exceptions. For a start, access to modern technology in the former USSR is from 15 to 20 times more expensive than in the US, while unskilled manual labour is significantly cheaper. Where does the competitiveness of the Russian economy lie? The more we are integrated into the world market, the greater the pressures on us to develop our 'strong' side – that is, primitive work for miserly pay. This is the usual kind of specialization that takes place in underdeveloped countries.

In the framework of this specialization maintaining modern production is burdensome and unprofitable. In East Germany those who lost their jobs following unification were not primarily the street-sweepers, but the skilled workers, engineers and technicians.

Modern-style workers are expensive. If there is to be work for them, large capital investments are required, and the profits take some time to start flowing. Today it is much easier to make millions out of common speculation, selling pies, pornography and horoscopes. We have no Protestant bourgeoisie thinking of God and the honour of the firm. The country's new owners have no need of skilled workers, who would pose a danger to the liberal project by being too educated, liable to demand humane working conditions and the right to participate in management, and likely to provide a lead to the unskilled workers, making their protests more organized and effective.

In the West such workers are bought off with high wages and social guarantees. It was on this basis that the traditional social democratic model was constructed. In Russia there is nothing to buy them off with. Thus in the free East European market the spade is more profitable than the computer.

In the circumstances, the free market is an obstacle to modernization, to the development of initiative and to innovation.

Notes

1. A part of the Free Democrats group headed by world chess champion Kasparov remained within Travkin's party, but the majority left and formed their own party, with a similar programme but a somewhat different organizational structure.
2. *Izvestiya*, 12 October 1990.
3. *Paritet*, August 1990, p. 5.
4. *Des Moines Sunday Register*, 12 August 1990.
5. This is no exaggeration. In the early months of 1991 the view was often heard among economic managers that the consistent application of a Polish-style programme in the USSR would precipitate a fall of as much as a third in productive output. One can surmise that the result would be to reduce consumption by large numbers of the Soviet population not just to 'typical' Third World levels, but to those of the poorer Third World countries.
6. *Arbeiterkampf*, 28 May 1990, no. 319, p. 8.
7. *Stolitsa*, 1990, no. 1, p. 37.

6

Is There an Alternative?
The Market, but What Kind
of Market?

At the end of the twentieth century no economy can dispense with market relations. But why should we regard the capitalist 'free' market as the only possible one, and bureaucratic centralized control as the only possible form of planning?

Liberals insist that the market ensures freedom of initiative. Unfortunately, for many initiatives the market turns out to be a no less serious obstacle than the bureaucracy. Private property, of course, broadens the opportunities open to the individual, meaning the individual owner of capital. What about the mass of the population, who will obviously never acquire significant capital?

What people with initiative need is not the market or private property, but the opportunity to realize their initiative. If this can be done through the market, fine. If through some other means, then that is fine too. Stalinist activists, the commissars of War Communism, early Christian preachers and biblical patriarchs, crusaders and Spanish conquistadors all had initiative, but what they were doing had no relation to the market or to capitalism. The 1930s saw a much higher level of active initiative than the epoch of perestroika, though the forms in which this initiative was manifested were at times totally barbaric. The conditions for initiative were created in the course of accelerated industrialization.

One can show 'initiative' in the building of concentration camps or the sale of bread rolls. The problem lies in deciding what kind of initiative society should encourage, in what forms, and through what methods. It is obvious that market mechanisms provide scope for particular types of initiative and impede others.

The problem society faces is not an abstract one of 'encouraging initiative' – if this were the case, we would give awards for theft – but

94

involves encouraging people to take part in activity which is in line with social priorities. In today's CIS the most urgent needs are for the renewal of health care, education and culture, the installation of modern and, most importantly, environmentally sound technologies, and the modernization of the infrastructure, the transport system and means of communication. All of these goals are either blocked by the free market, since they are essentially unprofitable, or they provide scope for the combination of 'market' and 'non-market' mechanisms.

The artificial suppression of market relations and the ban on entrepreneurial activity did nothing to expedite the growth of initiative from below. But the implantation of the market 'from above', and a policy of privatization carried out within the framework of the existing economic and social structure, are no better.

The paradox is that today, the policy of transferring state property into private hands is the most reliable guarantee that a real bourgeoisie will not be able to rise in a natural manner 'from below'. It will be crushed and subordinated by powerful bureaucratic capital. Today Russian entrepreneurs complain about apparatchiks who prevent them from working, placing administrative spokes in their commercial wheels. Tomorrow the very same apparatchiks, transformed into directors of super-concerns, will begin smothering entrepreneurs by economic methods. Admittedly, our new ideologues are correct on one point: economic methods are more effective.

What is occurring in the former Eastern bloc is not simply the formation of a new bourgeoisie, but several parallel processes. Three different bourgeoisies are emerging simultaneously:

1. A bureaucratic capital is rapidly taking shape. This is based on the transformation of the old totalitarian power into the new 'bourgeois property' (this in no sense means a division of government from property – the state and the new bourgeois oligarchy are joined together like Siamese twins).

2. A speculative-comprador bourgeoisie is forming around the foreign corporations which have established subsidiaries in the former Eastern bloc. This bourgeois sector is developing into a junior partner both of the foreign capitalists and of the home-grown oligarchy. These people are well placed to grow fat on the collapse of the economy; they profit from the maintenance of technological dependency and backwardness, which allows them to play the role of 'intermediary' between the primitive homeland and the flourishing 'Western world'.

3. Finally, there is a sector of modern productive-entrepreneurial capital, analogous to the 'national bourgeoisie' of the Third World.

The people in this sector are trying independently to build up their own businesses, to compete with Western firms, and to create products needed by society.

Of course only the third group is capable of making a positive contribution to the modernization of the country. But this group will not be able to develop normally within the framework of the liberal capitalist project. Large capital squeezes small capital, and the oligarchy in league with the state will have no trouble crushing competitors. The independent national entrepreneurial bourgeoisie would only be able to survive if it collaborated with a strong, democratically organized social sector, acting as its junior partner. Unfortunately, the destruction of the state sector is now proceeding at such a rapid rate that the prospects for the national entrepreneurs are also very unfavourable.

Liberal ideologues can always complain that what we have is an 'inferior', 'counterfeit', defective or deformed capitalism, but the problem is that under present circumstances a different capitalism, 'civilized and democratic, with a human face', simply cannot arise.

On the level of current policies, the rapidly growing gap between rich and poor means a new rise in social tensions, new strikes and acts of protest, and as a consequence, the need for efficient police repression if the reforms are to be successfully implemented. This is why the economic reform was so often postponed in 1990 and 1991. The authorities had not yet resolved on a full wage freeze and intended, at least initially, to grant workers compensatory pay rises. But such an approach could only worsen the situation. On the other hand it was quite clear that in conditions of rapid price rises this compensation would not prevent the living standards of a significant part of the population from falling. Simultaneously, the growth in wages would stimulate inflation, and one of the government's most important goals would simply not be achieved. Without doing anything much to improve the situation of the workers, such a reform promised to harm the very middle levels whose support for the transformations was being sought.

The most critical danger was that of unemployment. Under conditions of constant labour shortages most people are inclined to take this threat lightly. In the new circumstances, however, enterprises will not only be unable to create new jobs, but will be cutting back on their present staffing levels. The changed conjuncture will affect hired workers first. Literally in the space of one or two months a 'reserve army of labour' will take the place of the 'shortage of labour resources'.

Trying to lower the temperature of social conflict, the authorities may put pressure on the enterprises, forcing them to keep superfluous workers on the payroll. In this case, the worst possible choice will once again be made. Retaining an excessive number of workers will be unprofitable but unavoidable, while the workers will suffer both from the transition to the market and from the continuing ill-effects of administrative interference in the economy. In short, the plan-market economy 'CIS style'.

Among the first to suffer from the changes will be the nascent workers' movement. Having gained their freedom of action on questions of employment, the managers in most enterprises will immediately try to sack the 'troublemakers' who 'incite' labour conflicts and organize strikes. The history of world capitalism has allowed the ruling classes to accumulate an extremely rich experience of strike-breaking. It will probably be applied here in the near future, along with other kinds of Western expertise.

It is clear enough what the commercialization of education, health care, housing and science has in store for us. Scientists for a long time have been complaining about the shortage of funds for basic research, and about the growing 'brain drain' that has resulted. They note that in most Western countries and Japan scientific research is protected in one way or another from the action of market forces. It is precisely our developed system of free education and our system of social guarantees in the fields of health care and housing – of wretched quality, but at least reasonably well established – that have allowed our society to stay afloat in conditions of crisis and have allowed us to avoid becoming part of the Third World.

The 'Five Hundred Days'

Although ideological preparation for the transition to the capitalist market has been underway in the mass information media since the late 1980s, practical changes were a long time in coming. Liberal commentators and opposition deputies in the soviets constantly attacked the government for lack of resolution, while the government itself took one step after another in the direction they urged. Nonetheless, a decisive breakthrough had to await the events of August 1991 – and even then there were hesitations and second thoughts.

In the pre-August period this delay was due not so much to the ideological difficulties of Gorbachev and his Prime Minister Ryzhkov who then represented the Communist Party, as to fear of the social explosion that could follow if a programme implying rapid price rises, lowered living standards and the growth of social inequality were seriously implemented, and also to the lack of unity at the highest levels of government. This fear was to last up to August 1991 and was not wholly to be dissipated even then.

What was required for carrying out a sweeping programme of liberalization and 'stabilization' was a regime which was strong and resolute, and which, at least in the initial stages, enjoyed the trust of the population. Ryzhkov and Gorbachev had none of these prerequisites. Although in the spring of 1990 Gorbachev was proclaimed president of the country, technically with unlimited authority, he had no real power. The republican bureaucrats would not submit to the union government, the local apparatus was collapsing, and not even special laws could defend the authority of the president.

The 1990 elections to the republican and city soviets altered the situation dramatically. Boris Yeltsin become the head of the Russian government, Anatoly Sobchak came to power in Leningrad, and Gavriil Popov was elected president of the Moscow Soviet. In this way the liberal-populist bloc which had been formed during the previous summer at the Congress of People's Deputies of the USSR gained real power at key levels. The conditions for implementing radical pro-capitalist reforms from above had been brought closer.

A group of experts chosen by Yeltsin and led by Shatalin came up with the '500 day' programme, which was meant to come into effect from October 1990. This programme, which proposed to lead the country out of its crisis though the introduction of an austere market capitalism, proposed abolishing the state subsidies which guaranteed existing levels of consumption by the population, doing away with subsidies to loss-making enterprises, cancelling state capital invest-ments, 'liberalizing' – that is, raising – prices, and most importantly, carrying out massive, rapid privatization.

Since the authors of the plan did not envisage that the rapid price rises would be followed by an equally sharp increase in wages, the simulta-neous introduction of a rationing system was projected as the sole means of avoiding mass hunger. All the same, the norms for minimum consump-tion set out by the authors of the programme were laughably small.

After the liberal ideologues had spent several years accusing the Marxists of wanting to 'experiment on the living organism of society', the Russian government was preparing, in the name of implementing liberal ideas, to subject the population to the most grandiose social experiment since Stalin's collectivization. In the space of a few months the whole traditional way of life, including the existing economic relations and the imperfect but familiar system of prices and structures of production, was to be destroyed.

After all its declarations on the inadmissibility of centralized planning and state interference in the economy, Russian liberalism had presented us in practice with a harsh centralized state plan, drawn up in a matter of days.

These moves drew criticism even from moderate liberal economists. P. A. Medvedev, I. V. Nit, L. M. Frankman and I. I. Kharlanov published a collective letter declaring that the government had been carried away with enthusiasm for 'the administrative side of the matter', and was pursuing policies which would inevitably lead to 'social catastrophe'. While not objecting in principle to privatization, the authors of the letter stressed that in the existing circumstances the broad privatization foreseen in the programme would not only fail to increase economic efficiency, but on the contrary would lead to chaos.

> The system of directive planning is collapsing, centralized supply is falling apart, and market trade has not yet been established. To privatize enterprises in such circumstances means to deprive them either of supplies or of sales – that is, to condemn them to ruin. Political instability will aggravate the risk factor, turning any private investments into 'Russian roulette'.[1]

In fact, this was precisely what the project's backers had in mind. In such circumstances the only people who can invest money and buy up enterprises are those who have reliable political guarantees, and the only guarantee is power itself. In this way the ruling circles and above all the bureaucracy acquired the possibility of effectively monopolizing the right to private property, sharing it only with those people and groups who show loyalty and are willing to become the junior partners of the new owners.

The bureaucratic oligarchy were willing to exchange power for property, but were not prepared to divide it up. In essence, the programme of introducing capitalism 'from above' was aimed simultaneously at cutting off any natural growth of entrepreneurial capitalism 'from below'.

For the majority of the population the only role that remained was that of wage slave, or at best of client or assistant to the oligarchy. In these circumstances a social explosion was clearly inevitable. Those who were being moved to acts of protest included not only the lower orders of society but also a significant part of the middle levels, the people who initially gave their enthusiastic support to the idea of capitalist reforms.

Nit and his colleagues wrote:

> The authors of the '500 days' assume that the various strata will react peaceably to the measures outlined in the programme. But for them to suggest a 'temporary' lowering of living standards, while relying solely on agitation and propaganda to convince people to accept it, is simply not serious. The Soviet people know that there is nothing more permanent than such 'temporary' measures. At a time when the population is in an explosive mood, and has put its trust in the Russian leadership precisely on the basis of that leadership's promise not to allow any further worsening of mass living standards, such a course is suicidal. Starting out with such an orientation, they will not succeed in maintaining a popular mandate for the 500-day programme.[2]

For the moment, such a popular mandate allowed the new rulers of Russia – Yeltsin, Popov and Sobchak – to demand the introduction of their programme. Their resignations from the CPSU were symbolic gestures marking the end of the old regime. But Yeltsin and his followers continued to cultivate links with leading individuals in the party and in the security forces right up to the events of August 1991.

Throughout the countries of Eastern Europe the people were initially prepared to reconcile themselves to the difficulties thrown up by the liberal project, since they saw in this an inevitable price that had to be paid if they were to be saved from the discredited and hated Communist parties. The new authorities in Russia sought to present things in analogous fashion.

But the difference lay in the fact that whereas in Poland and Czechoslovakia the new governments were made up of former dissidents (which, of course, had not prevented the nomenklatura from acquiring property), Russia had witnessed only purely symbolic gestures by people who had never suffered serious persecution and who were of one flesh with the nomenklatura. Therefore, even the alleged 'salvation from communism' was not genuine.

The Russian government made use of the trust the people placed in it, and profited from the anti-communist mood of the masses, but these resources of trust were considerably less than in other East European countries. Trying its hardest to mobilize mass support for the 500-day programme, the Russian government and the Presidium of the Moscow Soviet led tens of thousands of their supporters on to the streets of the capital on 16 September 1990, demanding 'the prompt realization of the government programme' and the resignation of Ryzhkov, the then Soviet premier, whom they proposed to replace with someone from the group of Yeltsin or Popov. In fact, almost none of the participants in the meeting had actually set eyes on the 500-day programme. Even the deputies of the Moscow Soviet, and the Russian deputies who had not been elected to the Supreme Soviet, had been unable to obtain copies of the text. There had been no public discussion. The government clearly preferred to hide its true intentions from the public, replacing serious discussion of the imminent dangers with calls for 'taking a decisive step' and 'making the leap into the market', and warnings about the perils of 'stopping half-way'.

The programme could not have failed to arouse enthusiasm among those who stood to grow rich from the division of property. A commentator for the Moscow journal *Stolitsa*, observing the advent on the scene of the new Russian business entrepreneurs, wrote:

> This acquisitive fever reminds me of the old story in which it was decided to test the intelligence of an ape and an alcoholic. Both were put in empty rooms, from the ceilings of which were hanging a banana and a bottle of vodka respectively. A stick was placed in a corner. After trying to jump up and grab the banana, the ape worked out that it had to use the stick. But this thought never entered the head of the alcoholic. The experimenter prompted him, saying, 'Take your time, look around you, and think!' The alcoholic answered with the priceless words, 'What's the use of thinking? I need to jump!'[3]

Although the liberal propaganda that employed the clichés calling for a leap into the market could still bring people out into the streets, the liberal politicians themselves had no illusions about their chances of maintaining popular support. In the *New York Review of Books* on 19 August 1990 Gavriil Popov published a programmatic article with the striking headline 'The Dangers of Democracy', in which he explained that the participation of the masses in political life, attempts by the workers to defend their interests, and democratic liberties in general served to hinder the implementation of the reforms which the country needed. The implications of this were obvious: if the policies of market capitalism were to succeed, democracy had to be done away with. The Russian government, which had based its plans on the same economic philosophy of neoliberalism which has inspired Third World dictators, was bound to act in line with the political logic of the course it had chosen.

The ideological justification for repression had already been prepared. This was evident from the way Doctor of Historical Sciences A. Kiva declared in *Izvestiya* that those who would oppose the market included 'millions of drunks and layabouts', who would cry 'Help!

Save socialism!' Joining in this chorus, Kiva maintained, would be 'various slackers and social parasites'.[4] Of course 'Marxist fundamentalists will start howling at the top of their voices.' There is no point in standing on ceremony with such people, even if they number in the millions. In essence, the old arguments of the Brezhnev regime about individual 'backsliders' putting spokes in the wheel of society were being recycled on a new level. When *Komsomolskaya Pravda* in 1988 published its first programmatic article attacking socialists, it too spoke of attempts to organize left-wing drunks and layabouts to sabotage perestroika and organize strikes.[5] There it was still claimed that these people constituted a danger to socialism. Now, it was made clear, these same people threaten capitalism. The 'people' involved, of course, were the majority of the population.

The historian Kiva did not confine himself to describing the millions of 'drunks and layabouts' opposing the progressive reforms. Imagine, he added,

> what would happen if you journalists were to adopt a hostile attitude during the first, most difficult stages of the transition to the market, if you were to absolutize democracy, refusing to recognize the need to apply unpopular measures where these are indispensable.[6]

The circle had closed. We began with the condemnation of Red Terror, and we were finishing up with a justification of White Terror. The enemies of the new rulers were defined: millions of people were viewed by the ideologues of the new regime as 'drudges', 'lumpens' and 'drunks', journalists who were determined to write the truth, and left-wing intellectuals who still took the risk of defending the ideas of Marxism and socialism, while at the same time 'absolutizing democracy'. Where these people were concerned, 'unpopular measures' had to be applied.

Market Stalinism was passing from the realm of ideology to that of practice. But certain transformations were needed, of both a substantive and cosmetic description. The formation of a new oligarchy on the basis of the old nomenklatura was becoming a social fact. In place of the disintegrated totalitarian monolith an edifice of barbaric, authoritarian capitalist power was being erected. But before this new order could be consolidated there was a need to weld the state into a unified and authoritative instrument. So long as there were factional squabbles between Yeltsin and Gorbachev, or between Ryzhkov and Popov, it would be impossible to impose the new pattern.

Notes

1. *Argumenty i Fakty*, 1990, no. 33.
2. Ibid.
3. *Stolitsa*, 1990, no. 1, p. 37.
4. *Izvestiya*, 28 September 1990.
5. See *Komsomolskaya Pravda*, 31 January 1988.
6. *Izvestiya*, 28 September 1990.

7

Totalitarianism:
The Return of the Repressed

The Bulgarian historian Zhelyu Zhelev, who became his country's president after the proclamation of democracy, wrote on the totalitarian state that:

> During the dismantling of our Communist variant of the totalitarian system the regime in our country may degenerate to the level of fascism, as a less complete and less comprehensive totalitarianism. But for us such a fascism would represent a great step forward towards democracy! To the undeveloped or virginally pure political consciousness this might sound shocking and paradoxical, perhaps even offensive. But political illusions, emotions and prejudices are one thing, while political realities and the iron laws to which they are subject are another.[1]

Zhelev's prophecy threatens to prove more accurate than his readers might have supposed, even though none of the Eastern bloc countries has seen a Communist regime 'develop' into fascism through a process of natural evolution. The fascist threat has arisen not only, and not so much, in the bowels of the state as in the new social movement that has raised the banner of democracy.

There is nothing paradoxical about this. Just as the liberating slogans of socialism served as a cover for one of the worst totalitarian regimes in history, in Eastern Europe today a new anti-popular and anti-democratic power is forming under the cover of democratic ideology. This is no better justification for repression and for the crushing of civil liberties than the slogans of general liberation, and nothing is as effective at hiding corruption as pleas for the healing of society and for cleansing it of decay.

The psychology and structure of the new system of rule already begin to remind us of the psychology and policies of classical fascism, although the ideological basis has now changed. The new 'democratic'

regime in Georgia imposes a blockade on the rebellious city of Tskhinvali, and as a result new-born babies die in maternity hospitals which
are denied electricity. The 'offence' of Tskhinvali consists simply in the
fact that its inhabitants refuse to submit to the abrogation of their right
to autonomy. In Russia the idolization of Yeltsin is neither an accident
nor a hangover from old traditions, but a symptom of a new and
growing phenomenon. Elected bodies count for nothing and the man of
destiny rules by decree. And in case this man of destiny fails to make the
grade there are others waiting impatiently in the wings, among them
the Russian Vice-President Alexander Rutskoi and the leader of the
Liberal-Democratic Party, Vladimir Zhirinovsky. The leader of Russia's Liberal Democrats is, as one might expect, a rabid chauvinist and
Jew-baiter, but when he fulminates against the 'economic Chernobyl'
which Gorbachev and Yeltsin have sponsored people do listen.

It was entirely possible that in Russia, and even more so in various
countries of Eastern Europe, the democratic changes would turn out to
be no more than an intermediate stage, a transitional period in a
process of evolution from Communist totalitarianism to fascist totalitarianism. Some talked of Russia passing through a sort of Weimar
period. Only here, where 'virginally pure political consciousness' is a
sin, I am not ready to share Zhelev's optimism. One can hardly
maintain that the totalitarianism of Brezhnev and Zhivkov was worse
than that of Hitler. Of course, from the point of view of today's East
European liberals Nazism had indisputable advantages in that it rested
on private property which, as has been explained to us, is the only
possible basis for freedom and prosperity (especially in tropical Africa
or Turkey). But to address the question from another angle, it is hard to
convince people who are threatened with concentration camps of the
need for such 'progress'.

The danger is real. Not one of the East European countries today can
really be called a viable democracy. The ruling ideologies do not enjoy
the support of the population and the political institutions do not
express the interests of the majority, while the interests of small corrupt
groups appear at the centre of the political struggle. It is not surprising
in such circumstances that people are losing faith both in the new
regimes and in their leaders.

In November 1990 the newspaper *Demokraticheskaya Rossiya*
published the results of a survey of public opinion in Moscow which
showed that this was already happening. For the liberal politicians who
held power in Moscow, Leningrad (as it then was) and the Russian
republic, the results of the survey were not encouraging.

The rating of all the politicians with the exception of Yeltsin had fallen noticeably. Gorbachev, the liberal politicians aspiring to the role of 'democratic opposition', and even the leaders of the 'popular movement' were all losing the trust of the population. Yeltsin, it is true, retained a strong position in people's consciousness, but the popularity of the Supreme Soviet of the Russian Federation which he headed had fallen sharply. More than half the participants in the survey expressed dissatisfaction with the work of the 'democratic' Moscow Soviet, while the Supreme Soviet of the USSR was regarded in a positive light by only 18 per cent of respondents.

Only 26 per cent said they would vote for Gorbachev in a presidential election, and even Yeltsin received the support of only 33 per cent. For political parties of a right-wing liberal bent the results of the survey were also extremely discouraging, especially if one recalls that the poll was taken in Moscow, which these groups have regarded as their home territory. The extreme right-wing Democratic Party of Russia headed by Nikolai Travkin was obviously losing its original attractiveness for many of those polled, but nonetheless it held the leading position among the liberal organizations, clearly outstripping the more respectable groups. The Democratic Party received most of its support from unskilled workers and lumpen elements. There were reports of large monetary donations pouring into the Democratic Party from the *nouveaux riches*. However, the party was wracked by contradictions, and at supplementary elections for people's deputy in Moscow two rival candidates stood for the Democratic Party, flinging mud at one another.

Meanwhile, the more moderate or respectable liberal groups were finding that the ground was slipping quickly from beneath their feet. The popularity of the Social Democratic Party had fallen sharply. The former Democratic Platform in the Communist Party of the Soviet Union was also losing ground; this tendency was first known simply as the Democratic Platform, before renaming itself the Republican Party in November 1990 in tribute to its idol Ronald Reagan. As these two groups struggled to overcome their crisis they were forced to begin discussions on unification, but the attempts to establish a single organization provoked new internecine struggles within each of the parties. The few ideologically committed social democrats who had joined the Social Democratic Party wound up on the sidelines. One of the party's leaders, P. Kudyukin, admitted that a clear majority of members of the Social Democratic Party considered themselves liberals. Kudyukin and his supporters founded the Social Democratic Centre in an attempt to take their distance from the increasingly right-wing policies of the party leadership.

Sociologists began to talk of a crisis in the multi-party system. Yeltsin, gauging the situation perfectly, called on all democrats to unite in a single party under his leadership (he forgot that on leaving the CPSU he had pleaded the necessity that he should become the non-party president of all Russians). The call for everyone to unify behind a single leader was in line with the ideology and political practice of the Democratic Russia bloc, but its implementation was put on hold because of the inability of leaders further down the scale to agree among themselves. On the same day as Yeltsin called on everyone to unite under his banner, Telman Gdlyan announced the formation of his own People's Party. He did this in such a way as to leave everyone in total confusion, observing, to the consternation of his rivals, that it was his party which would serve as the basis for the national organization of which Yeltsin was speaking.

It was precisely the rivalry between 'democratic' leaders which for the time being saved the country from a new single totalitarian party. Gdlyan, Travkin and for some time Yeltsin dreamt of an 'all national' party, but fortunately for the country, they had been unable to agree among themselves on the division of ruling posts.

Meanwhile, the *Demokraticheskaya Rossiya* poll showed support for the Communist Party remaining stable but low. As an unexpected consequence of the disillusionment of the masses with liberals and 'democrats', support for the United Front of Workers had increased.

The neoliberals found themselves in an ideological trap. They enjoyed their greatest support among particular groups of technical personnel and among unskilled workers – that is, among precisely those people who were most likely to lose from the market. It was only to be expected that the most backward and demoralized strata of the population, who are most easily manipulated, would readily take the bait of liberal propaganda. But to consolidate the support of these sectors was impossible, since the liberal policies were aimed directly against their interests. The social base of the right-wing forces was thus extremely unstable, and was narrowing fast.

The *Demokraticheskaya Rossiya* poll also overturned the legend about the unpopularity of the word 'socialism'. Despite two years of intensive propaganda, only 27 per cent of people surveyed in Moscow – the citadel of liberalism – expressed support for 'modern Western capitalism'. Meanwhile 48 per cent favoured a socialist society, half of them endorsing the definition of socialism employed by the Socialist Party ('a society based on workers' self-management'). Supporters of 'communism' accounted for 3 per cent, while 7 per cent wanted a 'strong regime'.

The publication of such material in a newspaper which normally campaigned assiduously for neoliberal ideas was in itself something of a sensation. The wave of liberal euphoria began to ebb. The greater the ebb, the greater the decline in the hopes of the leaders of the new soviets that they could implement their projects using democratic methods. Addressing the Supreme Soviet in November 1990 Anatoly Sobchak demanded not only the banning of the Communist Party, but also the liquidation of all political parties, while Gavriil Popov insisted on the quickest possible abolition of the power of the soviets.

In arguing for his position, the Moscow ruler was forced to acknowledge publicly that capitalism was to be implanted in Russian using the same methods as Stalinist communism. The new system, Popov declared, did not 'arise in a natural manner out of the past'. It would have to be implanted 'in an artificial fashion, from outside, in the ploughed-up field of the previous social order. Denationalization and desovietization must be brought in from outside.' It was true, Popov conceded, that there were also gigantic differences; socialism had been introduced as something artificial, while the market would have to return as something natural. But in both cases the process itself was 'one of implantation, not simply of growth'.[2]

Meanwhile these remarkable natural processes, which had to be implanted artificially from outside for the benefit of the majority of the country's population, were serving to deepen the crisis, making barbarism and the collapse of normal life the norm. All this was accompanied, of course, by strident calls for a return – via an artificial road – to natural norms, to 'genuine civilization'.

A number of economists who are far from embracing socialist positions even began expressing alarm. Tatyana Koryagina, who was one of the first to speak of overcoming 'false' socialist ideas, declared after the first months of liberal experimentation that 'the economic reform has in fact become an arena in which foul political games are played at the population's expense.' In the opinion of Koryagina, who is convinced of the need for market reform, privatization in current circumstances will place property and power in the hands of criminal elements, with all the attendant consequences. It is precisely these elements who 'need talks on private property to begin, who need an accelerated transition to the market. And once again economists are found who will start serving the needs of the politicians.'[3]

Similar observations have been made by A.V. Danilov-Danilyan, I.V. Oleinik, P. Medvedev and other serious economists. Yesterday's defenders of centralized planning, writes Danilov-Danilyan, today mouth ritual praises of 'the stock exchange', 'share prices', 'the conjuncture', 'marketing' and 'management'. Why, he asks, 'must our country, which has been exhausted by decades of uncompromising struggle, be held hostage to the illusions of another generation of radicals, who dream of using the iron fist to drive the people into the kingdom of happiness?'[4] The answer, unfortunately, is very simple: because these 'new radicals' are only expressing the new interests of the old bureaucratic oligarchy, which has kept a firm hold on the levers of real power.

The Congress of Labour Collectives of the USSR, held in Moscow on 8 and 9 December 1990, adopted a resolution sharply criticizing the policy of privatization and emphasizing the right of workers to make their enterprises collective or state property, the sole forms of ownership which can guarantee the workers' right to participate in decision-making. Plant directors organized in the Union of Civilian Enterprises came out with a critique of privatization, and another powerful director's organization, the Scientific-Industrial Union headed by A. I. Volsky, also took its distance from the liberal course adopted by the government and opposition.

Following the first liberal experiments in Moscow and Leningrad, and the growth of social tensions in our country, even some members of the intelligentsia began to face the realities. A wave of ideological opposition to liberalism began to develop, despite the liberals' strict control over the principal media of mass information.

Trust in the slogans of the 'democrats' declined steeply. Out of habit, thousands of people still turned up to meetings in Moscow and Leningrad, but these gatherings could no longer be said to represent the 'voice of the people'. Surveys of public opinion showed that the speakers were no longer able to stir, or even to interest, ordinary people, who were concerned not with how the 'sovereignty of Russia' was to be realized, or with the form in which the 'indestructible union of free republics' was to be retained, but with much more prosaic matters: how to get money, how to feed their families, and how to find work.

Sensing that they had reached an impasse, both of the contending groups attempted in the spring of 1991 to rally their supporters. Gorbachev called a referendum for 17 March on the future of the Union, well aware that since his personal popularity, that of his government and that of the CPSU stood at around 10 per cent, this was his only way of obtaining the support of voters. But Yeltsin also called his own referendum on the introduction of the post of president of Russia. As expected, both referenda turned in positive results, and each leader was able to interpret the outcome as an expression of the undivided support of the people for his political course.

Gorbachev's position became still more ambiguous after the newly formed Communist Party of Russia headed by Ivan Polozkov effectively broke with the president and the government, attempting to pursue an independent course as an opposition body.

No escape from the impasse was found. Neither Yeltsin's calls for Gorbachev to resign, which were supported by the leaders of the Kuzbass miners, nor mass demonstrations of Yeltsin supporters under anti-communist banners were of any help. Political tension became the norm, and the country gradually lost hope that things would improve.

Not even the near-universal detestation for Gorbachev and his new Prime Minister Valentin Pavlov could improve the position of the 'democratic bloc', since its leaders were finding it more and more difficult to explain how their programme differed from that of the government. The crisis of the democratic movement in no way strengthened the position of the Communist Party. Ceasing to believe in the 'democrats', people did not have any particular illusions concerning the Communists; fortunately the experience of decades is not easily forgotten. This meant that neither Ivan Polozkov nor other leaders of the Communist Party of Russia were really able to exploit the possibilities opening up before them in the new situation. Nevertheless, their calculations were clear: they expected that sooner or later the mass of citizens, tired of the incompetence, irresponsibility, failures and corruption of the new democratic leaders, would return to the fold of the Communist Party, not because it was capable of offering them a better life, but for the simple reason that amid the collapse of the democratic movement the Communist Party might appear a 'lesser evil'.

As we know. the slogans and language of Communist ideology have been profoundly compromised. But in the course of two years the Russian (and also East European) democrats had managed to compromise the idea of democracy almost as thoroughly as the Communists compromised the idea of socialism in seventy years. The difference between the democrats and the Communists was difficult to discern – of course today's democrats were yesterday's Communists, not humble party workers but party secretaries and senior advisers.

Polozkov's Communist Party was not, of course, a party of workers. Nor was it a party of ideologues and bureaucrats. It was a party of bureaucratic business, with multimillion-ruble interests and practical experience of commercial dealings. Declaiming about the vices of the market, the Communist Party of Russia remained better prepared than anyone else in the country to profit from the defects of the new system.

The party criticized the system, and grew rich from it. While the democrat economists wrote about the necessity of privatization the party bureaucrats put the theory into practice. Both the democrats and the Communist Party of Russia encouraged nationalist feelings, despite the risks this entails. On this terrain, however, it is the democrats who have the advantage.

The 'democratic' leaders were stricken with fear at the prospect of a come-back by the Communists. The latter seemed poised both to exploit the new economic policies and to appeal to popular disaffection. Communists still have formal control of the state apparatus and security services. On the other hand the democrats have influence too, especially among functionaries who would like to emancipate themselves from the trammels of party control. The democrats began to ponder the advantages of the simple, radical expedient of outlawing the Communist Party and its ideology. A 'preventive' ban on the Communist Party might, of course, protect the country from a restoration of the old dictatorship – but at the price of establishing a new and perhaps more vigorous one.

What can be counterposed to the 'Communist threat' when faith in the new liberal myths and in the promises of the 'democratic leaders' is collapsing, and when the new post-communist democracy begins to display leanings towards an anti-communist fascist dictatorship?

There was clearly an ideological vacuum in the country. The objective need for a 'third force' was felt more and more acutely. The difficulty facing leftists, however, consisted in the fact that while presenting a political alternative, they did not manage to solve their numerous organizational problems, nor did they win a significant part of the intelligentsia over to their side.

The Socialist Party was one of several organizations whose influence began to increase during the autumn of 1990. Support for the Socialists came from the workers, and the party attracted least backing among the intelligentsia.

The sociologist Leonty Byzov, who can hardly be suspected of sympathizing with the left, was forced to acknowledge that 'the autumn provided a number of trump cards to the supporters of socialist self-management'.[5] As was to be expected, the Socialist critique of the ideology of the 'free market' found its greatest backing among skilled workers.

The Second Congress of the Socialist Party, held in Leningrad on 24 March 1991, showed clearly that while the Socialists might still be few and weak, their political influence was growing. Assessments of the conference in the press, including such hostile newspapers as *Kuranty* and *Nezavisimaya Gazeta*, testified to the fact that the mass media felt the Socialist Party had to be treated as a serious political organization, one which was quite different from all the others.

Nevertheless it was clear that although the Socialist Party and its allies had proclaimed as their objective establishing a third force in Soviet politics, they had not yet become such a force, and did not have much time to achieve their aim. Unless the movement for a third force succeeded in transforming the political situation, the hopes of democratic development would not be realized. Then, more than likely, the prophecy of Zhelyu Zhelev would come to pass.

Notes

1. Zhelyu Zhelev, *Fashizm't* ('Fascism'), Sofia 1990, p. 9.
2. *Ogonyok*, 1990, no. 51, p. 5.
3. *Literator* (Leningrad, 23 November 1990.
4. A.V. Danilov-Danilyan and I.V. Oleinik, *Kak strane nachat' zhit' luchshe* ('How the Country Can Begin to Live Better'), Zelenograd 1990, pp. 15, 23. See also L. M. Freynkman, *Za 500 dnei ili za 600 sekund* ('In 500 days or 600 seconds'), Zelenograd 1990.
5. *Demokraticheskaya Rossiya*, 1990, no. 5, p. 10.

8

The Time for Repentance

During the eighteen months up to August 1991 the old Soviet Union had been tottering. Crisis had followed upon crisis, meeting upon meeting, and one alarming rumour upon another. Nevertheless, it seemed that the only real changes that had occurred were an increase in the disorganization of production and a corresponding fall in living standards. Neither the promises of universal prosperity after the introduction of the mythical market, nor the steep increase in prices, nor the privatization of enterprises served to halt the collapse of the economy.

Referenda in the USSR, the Russian Federation and the Moscow municipality showed only that these consultations, which involved submitting vacuous questions to judgement by a disoriented public opinion, could solve nothing. Gorbachev won support for a 'renewed union', while maintaining a tactful silence on what it was he planned to renew, and how. Yeltsin obtained approval for the election of a president of Russia, neglecting to inform the public of the rights and functions which the new titular head would exercise. In analogous fashion, Gavriil Popov won support for his idea of direct elections for Moscow mayor, despite the fact that those who voted 'yes' to this proposal included both people who were anxious to express support for Popov, and others who saw direct elections as a way of getting rid of him.

The vacuous questions received meaningless or ambiguous replies. The political process was heading into a dead-end. Less than six months after the rousing 'yes' to a renewed union in March 1991, the still unrenewed union fell to pieces. Yeltsin's calls for Gorbachev to resign and Gorbachev's appeals for order, together with the appearance on the streets of crowds of people and military units, created a surreal spectacle that concluded in a surreal, make-believe putsch. When it is reported from some Latin American country that 'tanks are in the streets of the capital', people understand that a coup d'état or revolution has taken place. But when we heard the same about

Moscow, we understood only that military hardware had been paraded pointlessly through the streets before being driven back to base.

We were living in the world's largest theatre of the absurd, on a stage that made up one-sixth of the globe.

In July 1991 the popular Moscow weekly *Kommersant* carried as its front-page headline: 'The Crisis of Soviet Parliamentarism'. A sad statement, especially considering that the first relatively free elections in the country for seventy years had been held only a little more than a year earlier. *Kommersant* observed:

> In the middle of July, the union and Russian deputies went on holiday. Their departure was ignominious; both legislative bodies were in serious crisis. The Supreme Soviet of the USSR was finding itself increasingly on the political sidelines, while the Congress of People's Deputies of the Russian Federation had not even managed to choose itself a new president, and risked sharing the fate of the union assembly.

To this one should add the serious crisis, and indeed political paralysis, which even earlier had beset the Moscow and Leningrad Soviets. People were tired of the pointless squabbling and patent incompetence of deputies at all levels. There was disillusionment with the changes and with the inability of representative bodies even to counterpose alternatives to the unpopular measures being implemented by the executive authorities without the consent of the legislatures.

Summarizing the position, *Kommersant* stated: 'The executive power has grown tired of the legislative power.'[1] One could not help but recall the famous words that the sailor Zheleznyak flung at the deputies of the Constituent Assembly of Russia in 1918 when the Bolsheviks came to dissolve it: 'The guard has grown tired.'

It is curious that the new democracy which had existed in the USSR for only a little more than a year should already have been suffering from all the ailments of Western democracies while possessing none of their strengths. There was no mistaking the ineffectiveness of the representative bodies, the confusion over procedure, the conflicts between the various institutions of government, the apathy of the voters, the corruption among the politicians and the collapse of faith in political parties. The reason for this lamentable state of affairs was also obvious: the weakness of civil society, and its inability to act as a real basis for democratic processes.

The mid-1980s had witnessed the rapid growth of civil society, which had emerged through the grassroots formation of thousands of clubs, groups and associations which were often transformed into mass movements. Alas, by the beginning of the 1990s the picture had changed radically. Most of the clubs had either fallen apart, or were eking out a meagre existence, or had been transformed into the lower-level structures of large bodies linked to the authorities and organized along traditional 'vertical' lines involving strict hierarchical and centralized relationships. In other words, the civil society that had begun to arise in Russia had been smothered. This occurred precisely in 1989–91, when the whole world was talking about the creation of democracy in the USSR.

It was not only that the Democratic Union and the popular front movement had been unable to compete with the liberal-bureaucratic elite which in the final analysis had become the supreme ruler of the country's destinies. All of those who had pinned their hopes on the development of democracy from below and on the self-organization of society had suffered a defeat. The conflict between liberals and radical democrats, between the reforms that had been born in the corridors of power and those that had been dictated by the street, was sometimes covert, sometimes open and bitter (it is enough to recall the attacks by *Moskovskie Novosti* on the Moscow Popular Front and the Democratic Union and the no less hostile characterizations of semi-official liberals made in speeches by representatives of these organizations). The struggle continued throughout 1988 and a considerable part of 1989, finishing with the complete triumph of the elite, which managed to turn even street demonstrations to its political advantage.[2]

The losers also included the new parties which had come into existence during 1990. Most of these, as noted earlier, agreed totally with the ideology of the perestroika elite. Nevertheless, the parties contained hidden dangers. To a significant degree they had arisen from the grassroots, from the 'informal democracy'; their members could call the leadership to account, and influence the taking of decisions. The only exception was Travkin's Democratic Party of Russia, in which a harsh totalitarian discipline reigned and no discussion was permitted. Travkin, however, had founded this party solely for himself, leaving no place for other, much more influential leaders of the elite. Hence, Travkin's party was doomed as well.

The Democratic Russia movement suited the new political elite much better. Here the leaders were under no obligation to the rank and file. There was no system of accountability, and no guarantee of the rights of minorities. No one could query whether the actions of the leadership were in line with the programme and constitution, because such refinements simply did not exist.

When they left the Communist Party in 1990, Yeltsin, Popov,

Sobchak and the other leaders of Democratic Russia did not join new parties, and did not form their own. A situation arose that would be inconceivable in Western democracies; political parties were active only at the lower levels of the political system, while none of the serious politicians who were taking decisions and heading the executive and legislative organs were party members. Of course, this did not prevent these politicians from acting in a deliberate, concerted manner.

Russian society, completely unschooled in democratic politics, quickly lost interest in the parties, which were presented (including by the official-liberal press) as playthings of former activists in the informal movement, less than totally serious and quite unnecessary for the real political process. The largest such organizations had no more than four or five thousand members. Meanwhile, politics became more and more personalized; the public were taught to follow struggles between personalities instead of between ideas or organizations

Naturally, it was Yeltsin, the most popular and famous of the leaders of the anti-communist bloc, who managed to extract the greatest advantage from this situation. The Yeltsin mania, born even before the 1989 elections, reached its zenith following the election of the former Moscow party boss to the post of president of the Supreme Soviet of Russia in June 1991. On the streets of Moscow and other Russian cities exultant masses once again appeared with pictures of the leader. These crowds were an infallible argument against those who might have suspected the Russian government or the Presidium of the Moscow City Soviet of being undemocratic. 'The people are for Yeltsin,' activists of the Democratic Russia movement proclaimed triumphantly. The well-organized enthusiasm, along with carefully scripted expressions of mass indignation against numerous enemies who were weaving intrigues against Russia and its 'new government', were finally bound to convince the waverers. The 'voice of the streets', that was under effective control from the corridors of power, had come to serve as one of the government's arguments.

In earlier days, when Yeltsin was still a 'true Communist' and a 'fighter for social justice', one of his admirers used to bring a placard to meetings declaring 'Yeltsin is the Lenin of our time!' Readers may recall who was crowned with this accolade in earlier times. Out of the depths of the subconscious, from the 'historical memory', this ritual formula had surfaced. The 'Great Leader' Yeltsin had merged into a single being with the 'Great Leader' Stalin. Hopes for the 'firm hand' of a strong ruler and wise tsar, the totalitarian dream which for almost forty years since the death of the previous 'father of the peoples' had not found a worthy embodiment, had at last been fulfilled in the figure of 'Tsar Boris'.

Yeltsin's main strength was not, of course, the adulation of his subjects, but the deep, genuinely popular hatred for Gorbachev. It is difficult to imagine a man simultaneously detested by everyone, from professors to janitors, from Zionists to anti-Semites. Yeltsin embodied not only faith in the 'benevolent tsar' (or more precisely, 'wise despot') but also hopes of getting rid of Gorbachev.

As always in such cases, the hopes were illusory. Yeltsin was not only Gorbachev's most resolute and implacable enemy, but also his double. The resemblance between Yeltsin and Gorbachev was striking: the same reaction to problems, the same striving for power. Whenever difficulties arose, instead of looking for solutions, they both demanded additional rights, extraordinary powers and wider authority (as though Russia had ever suffered from weakness in the executive authority or from an excess of democracy!). The elections and the Congresses of People's Deputies were good for allowing the leaders to be 'legally' chosen as presidents of the Presidiums of the Supreme Soviets, for allowing them to be invested with extraordinary powers, and for opening their way to the presidency. But apart from this, such democratic niceties were merely an annoyance.

Gorbachev's road to the presidency was accompanied by real democratization and by ham-fisted reforms and other changes which made the lives of most people worse, though much more interesting. Goods disappeared from the shops, and a free press appeared on the streets. In short, there were some real achievements, though as always in our country these turned into national catastrophe.

Yeltsin's road to power was accompanied by unrestrained demagogy, by an escalation of promises, and by a complete lack of real action. An opposition that is deprived of power can readily be accused of 'unconstructive behaviour', but what were people to expect of governing authorities that behaved like an opposition? The levers of power in Moscow and in Russia were employed to the utmost, but with only one aim: to acquire yet more power.

Immediately after Yeltsin was elected president of the Supreme Soviet of the Russian Federation and the new Russian government was selected, the new authorities made it clearly understood that they considered their existing powers insufficient. As a result, Yeltsin received extraordinary powers, and later the post of president of the Russian Federation was created especially for him. Simultaneously, the posts of mayors of Moscow and Leningrad were introduced in order to strengthen the position of the new ruling group as they sought to create 'a system of direct executive power',[3] completely independent both of the representative organs and of society.

Few people were surprised when democratic slogans borrowed from Gorbachev's perestroika were used to try to justify the formation of this structure of authoritarian power. All democrats were ordered to unite in a single movement or party under the command of the leader Yeltsin, in order to carry out the sacred task of extirpating communism. The time had passed when Yeltsin, declaring himself the president of all Russians, had sought to be 'outside parties'. Now he stood 'above parties' but not 'outside' them; he had come to head all the 'democratic parties' simultaneously.

It is curious that among the intellectuals who were crying 'Hosanna!' to Yeltsin, no one appeared to have been struck by a bizarre contradiction: here was a democratic movement headed by a single, infallible leader. The role which intellectual 'fellow travellers' played in installing Stalinist totalitarianism in Eastern Europe in the 1940s is well known. They were needed by the regimes only until the situation stabilized and the new relations of power were consolidated. The erudition of the intellectuals, who were dreaming of remaking the world, served only to make the ideology of the authoritarian bureaucracy more attractive. Once this work was done, the fellow travellers were pushed on to the sidelines, or themselves became victims of the system.

The degree of loyalty which Yeltsin showed to his 'fellow travellers' can be gauged from the example of the miners. Orienting towards Yeltsin, the leaders of the Kuzbass miners shifted their economic and social demands on to the back burner, and concentrated on demanding the resignation of Gorbachev. They were not in a position to force the Soviet president out, something that Yeltsin's followers had understood perfectly when they provoked the miners to a political strike. Yeltsin and his aides not only manipulated the miners in cynical fashion but, as might have been expected, soon betrayed them. Forgetting the curses he had hurled at Gorbachev, Yeltsin signed an agreement to collaborate with the Soviet president even while the strike was still in progress. Turning up in the Kuzbass on May Day 1991, Yeltsin managed with relative ease to calm the leaders of the strike committees; these people were dependent on him, and no longer had a choice. But most of the miners were confused and indignant.

The intellectual fellow travellers of communism in the 1920s and the 1940s no doubt believed sincerely that they were acting for the good of the people. One can only guess to what extent the intellectuals of the 'Yeltsin team' were naïve, and to what extent they were cynical. Ultimately, it was no accident that Gavriil Popov and many other distinguished democratic politicians called for the use of a 'firm hand' to create a strong executive power, and that while speaking of 'dangers to democracy', they regarded mystical salvation through the 'introduction of the market' as much more important than strengthening civil freedoms.

To make a general judgement, the majority of the democratic politicians had already spied a niche for themselves in the projected system of the 'strong state', and did not worry unduly about the poor dupes who as a result of listening seriously to the leaders' freedom-loving speeches, were at risk of being heaved overboard from the Russian ship.

What we were witnessing in fact had little to do with democracy, the market or Russia, and everything to do with a number of much more specific concerns. The republican bureaucracy of Russia, which was weak but growing stronger, was trying to redistribute wealth and property to its own advantage, taking it from the central and party bureaucracy which was strong but growing weaker. Both groups dreamt of privatization, of appropriating the former party property, but the question of who was to become the new owner remained unresolved. For the bulk of the population this was an idle question, but for the participants in the carve-up it was of paramount importance.

The choice of terminology and slogans – the 'socialist choice' versus the '*sovereignty of Russia*' – was a matter of tactics. After all, not so long ago it had been Gorbachev who was preaching rapprochement with Europe on the basis of 'universal human values', embodied for some reason in Western liberal ideology, while Yeltsin was fighting for social justice and equality. The ideological roles had changed in line with the changing situation. The only thing which remained constant was the passion for dividing up property. Redistribution had taken the place of structural reforms. The redistributive psychosis united the declassed 'lower depths' and the bureaucratic elite.

'There is no other way!' the Yeltsin camp declared triumphantly, silencing doubters by saying: 'Whether Yeltsin is good or bad, we have no other leader and no other road.' No other road to where? And did it really make any difference whether it was a 'Communist' or 'democratic' oligarchy that led us to the bright future? In political terms these oligarchies were essentially identical; the differences were basically on the level of tactics, called forth by disagreements among the leaders on the question of who should get how much.

'Yeltsin's brilliant team', for which liberal newspapers expressed such rapture, was really a splinter group from Gorbachev's team which had brought the country to its state of crisis. While the leaders publicly reviled each other, functionaries migrated unconcernedly from one camp to the other. They knew very well that their tasks would be the same on both sides, and that the only things that would change would be their positions and salaries.

Meanwhile, the 'popular leader' was turning out to be far less popular than his role would have seemed to require. Prior to the elections, public opinion surveys showed persistently that only about a third of the population supported Yeltsin. True, this was far more than supported Gorbachev, who in the major cities could barely gather the support of 10 per cent of the population, but it was still clearly a minority. People naturally dreamt of getting rid of Gorbachev, who in the space of six years had led the country to collapse. But they were clearly reluctant to do this at the price of saddling themselves with Yeltsin, who might prove still more difficult to get rid of.

Before the 12 June elections for president of Russia the silent majority were in a state of perplexity. Did they really have only a choice between two evils? And how long would the silent majority remain mute? The answer was simple: until the major groups of workers managed to organize themselves, until strong trade unions and mass movements appeared, organizations that were genuinely independent both of the old 'Communist' oligarchy and of the new 'democratic' one. The first signs of such self-organization emerged in the spring of 1991 when students united, teachers went on strike, and the official trade unions began voicing independent demands, using the opportunity of the May Day demonstrations to condemn the policies of the 'centre' and of the Russian government simultaneously. Sober voices were also beginning to be heard in the press. The Greens and the Socialist Party tried to act as a 'third force', attracting more and more supporters to their side though their strength was still slight.

The results of the 12 June elections were not hard to forecast. Yeltsin received his presidential mandate, though in many industrial centres his vote was no more than 40 per cent. The so-called Liberal Democrat Vladimir Zhirinovsky – actually a demagogic Great Russian chauvinist – obtained nine million votes. Popov was elected mayor of Moscow at least partly due to the fact that at the last moment the Presidium of the Russian Supreme Soviet (in effect, Yeltsin) overrode the petitioning procedures legally adopted by the Moscow Soviet, replacing them with a new set that made it dramatically more difficult for independent candidates to be registered.

Only two weeks were allowed for pre-election campaigning. For the registration of candidates for president of the republic, 100,000 petition signatures were required; meanwhile, the candidates for mayor of Moscow had to present 35,000 signatures in place of the 10,000 originally stipulated. In the Moscow Soviet, the sad joke circulated that if Yeltsin thought 35 per cent of the population of the republic lived in the capital, he should assign it a third of the republican budget.

The abrupt change in the election procedures in Moscow was necessitated by the fact that the Socialist Party had unexpectedly named as its mayoral candidate the well-known economist and former leader of Democratic Russia, Tatyana Koryagina. Koryagina's election campaign was directed primarily at people who had voted for Democratic Russia in the spring of the previous year, but who had since come to suspect that they had been deceived. Koryagina and her candidate for vice-mayor, the Socialist deputy Alexander Popov, spoke of the need to stop the wave of corruption that was sweeping through state bodies, to put an end to privatization in the interests of bureaucrats and mafiosi, and to establish a genuinely democratic economy with a strong collectively owned sector. Koryagina's success could not help but arouse alarm in official circles. The journal *Nezavisimaya Gazeta*, founded by the leadership of the Moscow Soviet and, despite its name ('Independent Newspaper'), acting as the mouthpiece of the ruling circles, accused the Socialists of implanting a 'state of psychosis' in the country. Criticism of the authorities and protests against corruption, in the newspaper's view, were the main obstacles preventing the country from rising out of crisis and scoring successes on the world market. 'In both Chile and South Korea,' *Nezavisimaya Gazeta* argued, 'genuine capital appeared on the scene only after the appropriate political and economic conditions were established. What these conditions were, the whole world knows.'[4] In other words, nothing good was to be expected in the absence of a harsh Pinochet-style dictatorship.

Meanwhile, opinion surveys showed Koryagina holding a strong second position, suggesting that in a second round of elections she might have a chance of victory. In reality, she could hardly have hoped to defeat Gavriil Popov, who was backed by the extensive political machines of Democratic Russia and of the Moscow Soviet, as well as by state television and radio and by virtually the entire press. But the ruling circles of the Russian republic decided not to take any chances, and at the last moment introduced new electoral regulations. Koryagina, who had gathered 11,600 signatures, enough to satisfy the old provisions, was excluded from the ballot.

Yeltsin and his team triumphed. Now they had to put their programme into effect, handing out state property to bureaucratic groups and foreign corporations, introducing mass unemployment and slashing living standards. This was precisely what those who had supported him and brought him to power were demanding. But this meant that from then on the government's main enemy would be those millions of its beguiled subjects who on 12 June had voted for the next 'leader and teacher'.

The increasing personalism of Russian politics helped strengthen the position of the authoritarian populist leaders. Nonetheless, the organization that had been established in order to take power and seize victory in the elections was poorly suited to the new tasks of authoritarian-bureaucratic rule in conditions of total corruption.

After the stage of 'rocking the boat' came that of consolidating power. Yeltsin and Gorbachev began a quick rapprochement, affirmed in the joint protocol signed in Novo-Ogarevo by nine republican leaders and the president of the USSR. Then began the process of unifying the political apparatus of Democratic Russia with the section of the old party bureaucracy that had remained in the CPSU. One of the first orders Yeltsin issued as president was the decree on 'departization', outlawing the activity of the Communist Party committees in enterprises. However, this decree was not in any way directed against Gorbachev or the party hierarchs. Yeltsin himself stated: 'I opened a second front so that the reactionary forces that wanted to direct powerful volleys against Gorbachev would have to throw many of their resources on to this second front. And this is what has happened.'[5]

The organizations of the Communist Party were given until the end of 1991 to carry out their 'perestroika'. In reality, the decree was aimed primarily not at the Communist Party but at the trade unions – both old and new. Point two of the decree stipulated that trade union organizations should conduct their activity in the enterprises on the basis of agreement with the administration. If such agreement could not be reached, the trade unions would now find themselves outside the gate. At a time when mass sackings were being prepared, the purpose of this decree was quite clear.

For the various groups and factions of the bureaucratic bourgeoisie the time had come for open consolidation. On all sides, efforts were under way to accomplish this task. Democratic Russia leaders Gavriil Popov and Anatoly Sobchak joined with the most influential members of the Gorbachev group, Eduard Shevardnadze, Alexander Yakovlev and Vadim Bakatin, to announce the founding of the Movement for Democratic Reforms (DDR), on the basis of which a united democratic party was to be founded. In the view of the organizers, 'all of the democratic forces of Russia and of the Union' needed to merge in this

super-party, which in the words of Popov would 'devote the appropriate degree of attention to order and discipline'.[6]

The DDR was obviously intended as a 'bridge' to enable the liberal
section of the Communist nomenklatura to make the transition to new
structures of power. The newspaper *Kommersant* observed with its
characteristic cynicism that the former nomenklatura of the CPSU was
'forming a new democratic party' in which the old party elite could
'regroup once again'. Predictably, there were numerous problems. The
Kommersant report continued:

> The father-founders cannot agree on whether the party should be social
> democratic in character or whether it should immediately, without beating
> around the bush, declare for liberalism. However, this problem will most
> likely be solved in a very simple fashion. The party will raise the banner of
> social democracy – this is politically more expedient for former Communist
> leaders and ideologues making the transition to the new body – while the
> policies will be purely liberal, as representing the only possible course in
> present-day circumstances.[7]

It soon became clear that with anti-communism increasingly becoming the official ideology, even former Communist Party ideologues no
longer felt the need for a social democratic cover. In an interview in the
paper *Kuranty*, Yakovlev declared that in the course of the perestroika
period he had not only 'come to reject Marxism', but had also arrived
at the point of 'affirming the defeat of socialism'.[8]

Immediately after being elected as mayor of the capital, Gavriil
Popov set out to implement the policy of consolidation by forming a
'government of Moscow', and by choosing prefects from among the old
nomenklatura. The most odious figures involved were Bryachikhin, a
member of the Politburo of the Communist Party of Russia, and
Nikolsky, former second secretary of the Communist Party of Georgia
who was directly implicated in the bloody events of April 1989 when
paratroopers in Tbilisi cut down demonstrators with spades. This was
too much even for the generally docile press of the capital. *Moskovskie
Novosti* published an indignant article pointing to the past records of
the bureaucrats whom Popov had appointed. However, the politicians
who only yesterday had been describing the press as the 'fourth estate'
did not even deign to answer the critical voices of the journalist whom
they could no longer keep silent.

The main obstacle to the formation of a new super-party was not the
problem represented by the former ideologues of the CPSU, who
enthusiastically burnt the texts before which they had once forced

others to abase themselves, and who abased themselves before the writings they had once ordered burnt. The key hindrance was the existing structures of the democratic movement. The activists and functionaries of Democratic Russia were beginning to feel left out, and to fear that in the near future they would be replaced by tested apparatus cadres from the CPSU. The activists of the numerous democratic parties began to suspect the same. Nikolai Travkin, who at first had supported the DDR, later dissociated himself from it. The Republicans declared that the only basis for the unification of the democrats was the 'already existing structures of Democratic Russia'.[9] The Social Democrats took an analogous position. The leaders of the DDR did not drop their plans to establish a super-party. But it was now becoming clear that in the spirit of old traditions, the chief obstacle to the final triumph of the new ruling oligarchy was presented by the very forces and structures which had brought it to power. These forces had to be eliminated, or consigned to political oblivion. If the Liberal Democrats had shortly before helped the leaders of the oligarchy to clear the Socialists and informals out of the way, the same fate now lay in store for them.

Meanwhile, new bridges were being built for the old nomenklatura. One of these was the Democratic Party of Communists of Russia (DPKR), established by the vice-president of the Russian Federation, Colonel Alexander Rutskoi. The new vice-president was a colourful figure. A military aviator who had been awarded the title Hero of the Soviet Union during the war in Afghanistan, he began his political career in 1989 as one of the leaders of the Russian nationalists. Nominated by the organization Fatherland for the post of people's deputy of the USSR, he conducted a furious campaign against Western influences and against the selling off of Russia, but failed to be elected. Later he was elected to the Russian Congress of People's Deputies, again as a member of the bloc of traditional Communists. At the Congress, however, he experienced a sudden revelation, and as the leader of a whole group of turncoats, attached himself to Yeltsin. For this he was rewarded with the post of vice-president.

The DPKR was founded within the CPSU as an alternative to the official Russian Communist Party, and thus had the right to claim part of its property. The founding conference of the DPKR took place in August 1991. No special programme appeared that might have distinguished the DPKR from other democratic currents, and there was no political discussion. 'The sole point arousing what was not exactly disagreement, but rather a sort of confusion among the majority of delegates', noted *Kommersant*, 'was the retention of communism in the name of the future party.'[10] But no one was especially upset on this account, since the DPKR was clearly a temporary, transitional structure. Rutskoi himself indicated this clearly, declaring that in the near future the DPKR would 'integrate itself with progressive movements and parties', and above all with the DDR.[11]

Finally, Gorbachev's CPSU itself made up for past omissions. Early in August, *Pravda* published a new draft party programme that omitted virtually all mention of Marxism, hailed the end of 'the confrontation of social systems', and sought as quickly as possible to refashion the ideology and image of the CPSU to suit the liberal mood.

For hundreds of thousands of functionaries of the new and old power structures, this reconciliation of the elites was a propitious sign, a harbinger of peace and prosperity. For thousands of hoodwinked Democratic Russia activists and numerous members of the CPSU, it was treachery. For the country it was the beginning of a new epoch, in which democratic experiments would be replaced by serious, deliberate work on the construction of a new dictatorship.

Whether such a dictatorship could be installed and consolidated would depend critically on the degree to which the worker masses were able to counterpose their own interests and their own organizations to those of the new ruling groups. Few members of the Soviet intelligentsia saw any prospect of an independent labour movement emerging and playing an important role. At the beginning of the 1980s, when the whole world was following the struggle of Solidarity in Poland with surprise and admiration, Moscow intellectuals were complaining: 'Our workers aren't capable of that!' To be in opposition was perceived as the fate of writers and other highly educated people, who were alone capable of understanding the advantages of democracy. Meanwhile, the shortage of creative freedom was presented as the only shortage around which a serious struggle might be waged.

As always in such cases both the dissidents and the ruling elite, who agreed totally with these views, failed to understand the real processes that were unfolding. By the beginning of the 1980s surveys of public opinion not only bore witness to the acute discontent of the masses, but also showed that the ideas on life and society of skilled workers differed little from those of the Moscow intelligentsia. As a result of twenty years of the 'politics of stability', soon to be renamed 'stagnation', our society found itself – though only briefly – in an unprecedented state of agreement.

When the 'epoch of stability' gave way to the years of discord and decline known officially as 'perestroika', the intelligentsia gained an unprecedentedly broad audience. In the declarations of writers and the speeches of scholars people recognized their own fears, their own dissatisfactions, their own protests. Then, thousands of people who were not burdened with university degrees first took part in street demonstrations, and later began going on strike. The liberal press and opposition politicians, overcoming their initial astonishment and alarm (a glance through publications of 1988 and 1989 shows that these were their first reactions) promptly began to speak of the 're-awakening of the working class', which was giving proof of its 'political maturity'. Here was yet another mistake.

Although the workers' movement has in fact passed through several stages since the late 1980s, it cannot be described as having 'matured'. The first stage of the new Soviet workers' movement was the 'workers clubs' established in the enterprises – or more precisely, outside them – in 1987 and 1988. These clubs differed little from the other informal talking shops, and their participants had more in common with their brother informals than with their brother workers. In most cases the members of these clubs did not enjoy any authority in the enterprises, and their participation in the 'informal movement' was important only insofar as it meant that the leaders (including the present author) could reject accusations that the movement consisted only of intellectuals giving the proud response: 'No, we have workers too.'

It is indicative that when in 1989 strikes finally broke out in the mining regions, the local informals, including the workers' clubs, did not play any significant role in organizing them. In our labour movement each new stage generally begins with disparaging and rejecting the results of the preceding stage – one more symptom of immaturity.

The miners' strike of 1989 proved a turning point. This was a classic strike that involved many thousands of workers in an elemental process of self-organization. City squares in the mining districts saw endless meetings in which people talked for hours about their grievances (it was unexpectedly revealed that the miners, who had seen a good many conferences and congresses, could speak just as well as academics). A process of direct democracy arose, with the square demanding hourly accounting from its leaders. A ban on alcohol was introduced by the strikers themselves, and was willingly observed: in short, a situation which would have gladdened the heart of a revolutionary of 1905. Only one thing was lacking: the strikers did not have a political ideology. Nor could they have had, since there was no political organization.

The movement began, so to speak, in a vacuum. The traditions had been lost, and the official trade unions were hostile and impotent. The

strike committees of 1989 became the first form of workers' organization for sixty years – the first form, but far from the optimum one.

The strike committees immediately became burdened with numerous conflicting obligations. During the strike they became in effect the
sole real power in the mining regions, and even after the strike they
retained many important functions. As a result, the activists of the
strike committees became bogged down in petty administrative tasks
for which they were completely unequipped. At the same time, in the
absence of a workers' party, they were obliged to wage a struggle for
the political defence of workers' interests and to act as trade unions,
since the official trade unions refused to perform this role.

The strike committees, which soon took on the name of workers'
committees, were simply unable to cope. Moreover, none of the
primary structures of a labour movement was established. The activists
who had appeared in the burning days of the summer of 1989 moved
quickly into the city and regional strike committees. In addition, the
people who emerged as leaders at the strike meetings were not those
who had established their authority through longstanding participation in the movement – there had been no movement – but in many
cases, those who had simply shouted loudest. The leaders of the strike
committees began to be invited to the Kremlin, to be paid salaries for
participating in the work of the commissions that were overseeing the
fulfilment of the agreements between the government and the miners,
and to be invited to foreign countries including the US, Britain and
Argentina. Politicians of all shades, who had shown little interest in the
problems of the coal industry before the strikes of 1989, began to court
the miners, trying to attract them to their side.

As early as the autumn of 1989, the workers' committees found
themselves in crisis.

Initially, the miners did their best to avoid politics. They were
reluctant to provoke the party authorities, and were fearful of becoming the playthings of the Moscow leaders of one or another tendency.
However, avoiding politics proved impossible and was not how to
achieve authentic political independence. Lacking a grasp of the main
political questions, the miners were drawn against their will into
numerous political conflicts. Their unwillingness to engage in politics
meant that the miners became pawns in political transactions between
other forces. Through their hatred for Gorbachev and his team, whom
they considered responsible for the collapse of the country and for the
fall in workers' living standards, the workers' committees were automatically pushed into the embrace of Yeltsin and his circle, even though
their social and economic programme promised nothing better.

Among the leaders of the workers' committees, wariness towards the Moscow politicians and intellectuals came to be replaced by unthinking trust. To a certain extent, the composition of the workers' leadership changed as well. In their relations with the liberal deputies from the capital, the leaders of the workers' committees began to behave just as the worker members of the Moscow informal clubs had behaved towards the club leaders in 1987 and 1988. They became more like their new-found friends than their worker comrades.

The attempts made during 1990 to establish mass workers' organizations were not crowned with success either. The Confederation of Labour that was proclaimed in Novokuznetsk during the summer of 1990 proved unviable, since it contained miners' committees with small workers' clubs which through some miracle still survived. These structures were of very different social weight, and did not in any way complement one another, since they all suffered from related weaknesses. Some of them could not yet mount a real defence of workers' interests, while the others had already lost this ability.

Small independent trade unions had come into existence even before the miners' strikes, and after the events of the memorable summer of 1989 they began sprouting like mushrooms. All of them, however, remained small, and many were involved less in trade union activity than in business. An exception was the Independent Union of Miners (NPG), established on the basis of the workers' committees. However, the NPG could not boast of great successes either. The majority of workers remained in the old trade unions, since these provided access to various social benefits, while the new trade union centres could not.

Scandals began breaking out around cases of corruption. The most important of these shook the NPG during the summer of 1991, when union president Pavel Shushpanov was accused by his colleagues on the executive bureau of improper use of union funds and of failing to keep financial accounts. Investigations revealed everything one might have expected, knowing the state of affairs in the union – and a great deal more, which not even critics of the leadership had suspected. A commission of inquiry found that money had been transferred to an account held by the NPG in a failing commercial bank, in order to conceal it from creditors. Accounts had not been kept of hard currency donations from miners in other countries, and the families of union leaders had been living in Moscow at the union's expense. On learning of these abuses, the executive bureau withdrew Shushpanov's right of first signature, depriving him of the ability to dispose of union funds.

At this point a mine disaster occurred in the Donbass, and thirty-two miners were killed. Despite an acute shortage of funds, the union signed over 32,000 rubles to the bereaved families. Then Shushpanov appeared on the scene and, criticizing his 'tight-fisted' colleagues for valuing the life of a miner at no more than 1,000 rubles, handed over a further 300,000 rubles to the families. Where the union president had obtained such a sum remained a mystery even to other NPG leaders. A split occurred in the organization, and the miners became demoralized.

Commercialization became the scourge of the new unions. Many of them were formed on the basis of co-operatives, and included in their ranks both hired workers and their employers, violating the international principles of the free trade union movement. Other unions became so much involved in commercial activity that they showed little interest in the needs of their members. In the summer of 1991 the Russian Ministry of Justice refused to register the trade union body Sotsprof on the grounds that it was not a labour union, but a business combine acting under a trade union banner.

Another attempt at uniting workers was conducted through the structures of the Union of Labour Collectives of the USSR. The Councils of Labour Collectives, which had joined with the workers' committees to form this body, were as a rule representative but ineffective. The formation of the Union of Labour Collectives was provoked by the government itself when it tried to eliminate the councils – which had earlier been established by the authorities – because they might have presented an obstacle to privatization. The councils reacted angrily, and at their congress adopted a resolution against privatization. They also established links with the Yeltsin group, which had promised to retain the organs of self-management despite the fact that its programme envisaged even broader privatization.

The formation of the Union of Labour Collectives aroused great hopes, but the body suffered the same fate as the Confederation of Labour. Without proper institutions or its own ideology, lacking cadres and grassroots activists, the union failed to take off. The Councils of Labour Collectives, which had been established from above, rapidly proceeded to collapse. The leaders of the Union of Labour Collectives were either drawn into the fight to ensure the survival of the councils in the workplaces, with no hope of developing co-ordinated activity on the scale of the country as a whole, or simply had no idea what to do.

The miners' strikes of the spring of 1991 highlighted all the problems at once. While the liberal press wrote triumphant articles about the miners, the movement was in profound crisis. The government was no longer scared of strikes. Mass solidarity actions did not eventuate. Industrial enterprises went on strike here and there, but these stoppages had nothing in common with the actions of the miners. Sharp differences were apparent between the main mining regions, the Donbass, the Kuzbass, Vorkuta and Karaganda.

A mass movement of working people can only come about if there is unity among the industrial workers. A new wave of strikes in large industrial enterprises shows that this is possible. Actions by workers at the Moskvich car factory and at the Lyublinsky Foundry and Mechanical Works have shown that people are tired of waiting and are ready to defend their interests. The rise of the movement here has not been as rapid as among the miners, but this is not necessarily a bad thing. It now seems likely that the struggles of the miners will not have been in vain. New leaders are appearing, such as Vladimir Minaev from the Lyublinsky works, whose participation in the labour movement predates the first strike. The working class is beginning, though only beginning, to relearn its history. Economic chaos and the collapse of enterprises are combined with the complete unwillingness of those in power to defend workers' rights in any way whatsoever. The threat of unemployment on a monstrous scale hangs over the country. Living standards have gone into free fall. The only force that could hope to alter the course of events would be an organized and genuinely independent movement of working people – independent not only of the Communists, but also of the 'democrats'.

Throughout the world the main organizations of workers have been the trade unions. Socialist parties have grown and gathered strength precisely as a result of their links with the trade union movement. Among us a paradoxical situation has arisen. We have the largest working class in Europe, with the largest trade unions – which are among the weakest anywhere on the continent. It has only been since the middle of 1991 that this situation has slowly begun to change.

While the press was reporting in detail on the formation of new trade union groups with a membership of a few tens or hundreds of people, slow and complex changes were unfolding within the official unions. These were not always changes for the better. The official unions took on the name of the Federation of Independent Trade Unions of Russia (FNPR), but this did not mean they became workers' organizations. Rather, the FNPR leaders appeared ready to work for new bosses; instead of giving their allegiance to the Communist Party, the FNPR leaders now march under the banner of the Russian government, with which they painstakingly co-ordinate their actions. At lower levels within the union, however, genuine renewal was taking place. At the level of the workshops and enterprises there are now large numbers of new union leaders, elected by the rank and file since 1989 and very different from the old-style bureaucrats. The leadership of the Moscow Federation of Trade Unions and of other union federations has also undergone substantial changes.

At the May Day demonstrations of 1991 people carried placards condemning the policies of both the 'centre' and the Russian government, while from the top of the Lenin mausoleum, where Gorbachev stood glumly without being called upon to speak, the workers were addressed by Socialist Party Deputy to the Moscow Soviet Alexander Popov. It had become possible to hope that real changes were occurring in the labour movement.

With the looming threat of mass unemployment, the leadership of the Moscow Federation of Trade Unions had to take steps that were more than just symbolic. By the summer of 1991 it had become clear that a break with the leadership of the FNPR was inevitable; in this dispute, the trade unions of the main industrial centres sided with Moscow. Within the union leaderships, people began to suggest that the time had come to establish a party based on the labour movement. The first steps in this direction were taken in July 1991, when the Confederation of Anarcho-Syndicalists, the Socialist Party and the Moscow Federation of Trade Unions held a conference at which plans were revealed for the formation of a united political organization 'of the labour party type'. Those who spoke out in favour of the project included Tatyana Koryagina, the well-known economist and campaigner against corruption, and newly elected President of the Moscow Soviet Nikolai Gonchar.

The creation of a Party of Labour was a pressing necessity in a country where virtually all of the political groups, including the Communist Party, had opted for an ideology of 'free enterprise' and privatization instead of mounting a struggle for the rights of workers. But a Party of Labour could become a real force only if it rested on the trade unions and mass social movements, not just in Moscow but throughout the USSR, and only if the trade unions themselves carried their promised internal reforms through to completion.

The crisis in the miners' movement and the divisions in the ranks of the old trade unions testified to the changes that were taking place. New trade union structures remained to be built, and the political organization of the workers had scarcely begun. There was no time to be lost. The country was sinking into economic chaos; production was declining, the financial system was nearing its final collapse, enterprises were shutting down, and real incomes were falling precipitately. The interests of the majority of ordinary people, who possessed neither accounts in foreign banks, nor power, nor connections, nor property, could only be defended in such circumstances by strong and radical mass organizations, capable of resolute action.

In the absence of such organizations, the inevitable shake-out as the central and Communist Party apparatuses were finally replaced as the country's ruling institutions took the form of a bizarre, muddled farce in which the great majority of the population were bemused onlookers rather than participants. The denouement began on 19 August 1991. The radio and television reported that a State Committee for the State of Emergency had been formed and that Gorbachev had temporarily been removed from power. For some reason communications and transport worked normally, and the soldiers did not have ammunition. Yeltsin was not arrested. Although the events of 19 August were afterwards termed a 'Communist putsch', the official structures of the CPSU played no role in what occurred, and the declarations of the 'junta' were ideologically neutral. All of the putschists were intimate collaborators of Gorbachev; Prime Minister Valentin Pavlov was personally responsible for implementing the economic reforms. The active leaders of the Stalinist forces, such as Nina Andreeva and the Moscow Soviet deputy Ampilov, condemned the coup.

The evidence suggests that the members of the State Committee for the State of Emergency hoped to be able to seat Yeltsin and Gorbachev at a conference table and to establish a government of national unity in which they themselves would have the decisive voices. Materials which later appeared in the press suggested that these plans had been worked out in one form or another with Gorbachev and Yeltsin themselves.[12] But against the expectations of everyone involved Yeltsin decided on a different scenario, choosing to assert his own leadership rather than to engage in a new compromise.

Notes

1. *Kommersant*, special monthly supplement, July 1991, no. 30.
2. See B. Kagarlitsky, *Farewell Perestroika*, London 1990.
3. *Kommersant*, 1991. no. 26.
4. *Nezavisimaya Gazeta*, 13 June 1991.
5. *Izvestiya*, 7 August 1991.
6. *Rossiya*, 1991, no. 26, p. 2.
7. *Kommersant*, 1991, no. 26, p. 11.
8. *Kuranty*, 6 August 1991, no. 147. p. 1.
9. *Rossiya*, 1991, no. 26, p. 2.
10. *Kommersant*, 1991, no. 31, p. 3.
11. *Rossiya*, 1991, no. 26, p. 2.
12. See *Kommersant*, 1991, no. 34, *Solidarnost*, 1991, no. 11, etc.

9

The Coup that Worked

What actually happened? Why did the State Committee for the State of Emergency act so carelessly and tolerantly, at least in the first few hours? In any coup, the first five to ten hours are crucial. With hindsight, attempts have been made to explain away the strange behaviour of the committee through incompetence, slovenliness and lack of preparation. But Yeltsin himself has maintained that the coup was a year in preparation.

The junta also included the head of the KGB, Kryuchkov, who personally took part in the preparations for the military coup in Poland in December 1981, a coup that was impeccably organized and executed.

Every schoolchild in this country who has read Lenin's *Marxism and Insurrection* knows roughly how to bring about a coup d'état. The old heads of the KGB knew this better than any, having not only studied but also organized, numerous coups all over the world. And even with all the shortcomings of this department, it is hard to imagine professionals making such elementary mistakes at every step.

Above all, it is beyond comprehension why, in the early morning of 19 August 1991, the White House was not seized, and why Yeltsin, Rutskoi and Silayev were not arrested. The committee had a good few hours to do this. If Yeltsin found out about the coup at eight in the morning, then the junta actually had five hours to seize and occupy the White House. But even after this, they could have easily blockaded it and stopped its lord and master from getting there, thereby cutting him off from his control room.

After Yeltsin had enthroned himself in there, no one tried to shut him up inside. Neither the phones nor the electricity supply were cut off, and people were free to enter or leave.

Even Manezh Square was not blocked off, although it had been by Gorbachev the previous spring. No one tried to block off the city centre, to disperse the demonstrations, or even to check people's documents.

The television channels under the control of the putschists behaved strangely. Viewers were kept up to date on Yeltsin's movements and the protest demonstrations. Yeltsin's strike appeals were read out on the Metro, which, in response to the committee's orders, closed at 11.00 a.m. with the introduction of a curfew.

The most amazing thing is that the troops were not armed. The armoured cars did not have full complements, and even the officers had had the cartridges removed from their personal arms, which goes beyond the bounds of normal military practice.

It is not surprising that the majority of Muscovites treated the coup less than seriously from the very start. Children climbed over the tanks and people walked in the streets. They not only ignored the curfew, but did not even obey the traffic regulations.

Then there arise questions of another order: what was Yeltsin doing on the morning of 19 August? Did he really make no attempt to contact the authorities through the government communications system, which was working perfectly well? And if he tried, to whom did he speak? Why was there a gap of a few hours between the start of the coup and 'Tsar Boris's' public appearance as the fighter against the 'bloody junta'?

As far as Gorbachev is concerned, things also remain unclear. When he returned from the Crimea, he spoke of a blockade round his residence and of warships that guarded him from the sea. But it soon became clear that the president was not telling the people the truth. Eye-witnesses maintained that nothing out of the ordinary took place around Gorbachev's dacha at Foros from 19 to 22 August, and that everything, on the outside at least, carried on as normal.

Nezavisimaya Gazeta (the 'Independent Newspaper') has already accused Gorbachev of complicity in the plot. But if the president of the then Soviet Union was mixed up in it, what of the president of Russia? At least Gorbachev was cut off from the world at Foros, but Yeltsin remained free.

For some reason, no one has asked what Tizyakov was doing as a member of the junta. There was Pavlov, the prime minister, Yanayev, the vice-president, who had taken over as head of state, Kryuchkov and Pugo, the heads of the repressive organs of power, all front-line figures. But how did Tizyakov, a factory manager, worm his way into their company?

The fact is that Tizyakov was one of the deputies to Arkady Volsky, the head of the Scientific Industrial Union. The SIU is not only the largest association of top managers in the country, but also an organization that kept close contact with both Yeltsin's and Gorbachev's groups at the same time.

Naturally, the SIU condemned Tizyakov, but only on 22 August, when the coup had already ended. It is curious that after this, the official press tried to keep quiet about Tizyakov – and in the television coverage of the coup, he was hardly every present. It is not difficult to guess that Volsky himself would not have joined the coup. It was not worth him getting his hands dirty and, anyway, the risk was too great. All the same, a place in the junta was reserved for the SIU. And there were also political 'bridges' connecting the junta with other groupings in the ruling hierarchy.

Since 22 August there has been a new version of events put out by the ruling circles to explain what happened. It boils down to this: the putschists were simply trying to copy the coup of 1964 that removed Khrushchev. But, alas, there is no evidence to support this. The putschists knew full well the difference between 1964 and 1991, and they were working to a completely different scenario.

It was no accident that there was no attempt to call an urgent meeting of the Communist Party Central Committee, remove Gorbachev from the post of General Secretary and lean on the party structure at the centre and in the provinces.

The epidemic of strange 'suicides' of top officials, starting with Pugo's suicide completely out of the blue in the last days of the putsch, cannot fail to have aroused suspicion. The only people who commit suicide are those who know too much. And it was not by chance that Kryuchkov said in an interview on television after his arrest that he was in perfect health.

The well-informed paper *Kommersant* raises the possibility that Yeltsin was involved in the plot. According to its columnists, Yeltsin's courage and cunning bear witness to this. He provoked his opponents into doing it, and then crushed them, solving all his problems and ending communism in one go. The problem with this theory is that it makes the putschists out to be too stupid. But if they were so naïve as not to cut Yeltsin's telephone off, we could quite easily assume that they had let him deceive them.

Yeltsin was sure of success. He undoubtedly knew, at least on the morning of 19 August, that the White House would not be stormed. Either the appeal to the people to come and defend the White House was a huge practical joke, or, if Yeltsin actually feared a storming, a downright unscrupulous act. An unarmed crowd could never withstand a storming. It could only die under the tanks.

Nevertheless, the defence of the White House had great psychological significance. It had to be shown that unarmed people had overcome the putschists. It is difficult to understand that Yeltsin could have risked the completely senseless mass slaughter of hundreds of people without prior knowledge of the putschists' plan. How could he have found out? Most likely from the putschists themselves.

It is actually easy to find the answers to these questions in the junta's press conference on the evening of 19 August. In saying that they were going to come to an agreement and co-operate with Yeltsin, that Gorbachev would return after the restoration of order, and that economic policy would continue as before, Yanayev and his colleagues were speaking the complete truth. They were acting according to the planned scenario and were waiting for the others to make similar moves.

It is not difficult to guess that the putschists needed to have a sound basis for such certainty. Serious people such as Kryuchkov, head of the KGB, and Pugo, minister of the interior, would never have embarked on a coup d'état without finding out who would support it and who would remain neutral. They would certainly not just have supposed that Yeltsin was prepared to remain neutral in the event of a coup; they would have actually *known* it.

The putschists reasoned that, after the coup, there would have to be negotiations and compromises, and the creation of a government of national unity, including Yeltsin, or people from his circle. Most probably a few, of the junta would have had to drop out at this point, though the key figures, Pugo, Kryuchkov and perhaps Pavlov, would remain. It was not just a chance initiative by Nazarbayev, the president of Kazakhstan, to put himself forward as a mediator, as he was absolutely certain that there would be talks in the near future.

Meanwhile, Yeltsin chose a different scenario. Not only did he condemn the putsch outspokenly, but he began to act. While the junta carried on with the pretence of the coup, Yeltsin was bringing it to a conclusion by demanding, contrary to the constitutions of the then USSR and Russia, that all the power structures on the territory of the republic should be put under the control of his government.

This signified the virtual and irreversible dissolution of the Soviet Union on 19 August. It also rendered meaningless any attempt to recreate the Union on the basis of the agreement put together by Gorbachev. It meant the end of the power-sharing that had been secured in the constitution, and the start of absolute rule by Yeltsin.

When the junta realized what had happened, it was already too late. Sensing that it was going wrong on 20 August the members tried to take real power and call fresh divisions into Moscow, but these now ignored them.

To all appearances, a split developed in the junta. Yanayev sensed the others were trying to deceive him and make him into a scapegoat, and Kryuchkov and Pugo tried to take action. When the head of the All-Union State Radio and Television company, Kravchenko, arrived at the behest of the junta, he came across a strange scene. Yanayev demanded a broadcast to say that nobody was going to storm the White House, but Kryuchkov and Pugo said angrily that, if they had already been declared traitors and criminals, then they had no other choice than to act accordingly. Obviously, Yeltsin's stance had come right out of the blue.

It is not entirely clear why the putsch did not collapse on the evening of 20 August. The putschists remained inactive, quarrelled, and tried to prepare new subdivisions for battle, notably the 'Alpha' anti-terrorist group of the KGB, but their appeal was rejected.

Yeltsin and his team sat idly by and waited for something to happen. What? A storming? But the putschists no longer had reliable forces to accomplish this. Were they waiting for clarification? But the White House was kept well-informed of what was going on.

It is difficult to shake off the thought that they were waiting for the first blood, the expiatory sacrifice that would justify the subsequent repression not only of the immediate organizers of the coup, but also of the political opponents of the new regime.

And blood flowed on the night of 20 and 21 August during the clash between an armed column in the process of restationing itself, and a crowd at some distance from the White House.

Three died. At first, this incident was proclaimed as an attempt to storm the White House, but after a few days the official propaganda was forced to concede that there had been no storming. On the other hand, it was now possible to talk of 'the bloody junta', about the battle 'on the Moscow barricades'. The short-lived defence of the White House has been accorded officially recognized legendary status, just like the seizure of the Winter Palace by the Bolsheviks in 1917.

The putschists fled, though for some reason not to Iraq or North Korea, but to Gorbachev in the Crimea, where they were successfully arrested. Yanayev, Pugo and Kryuchkov's coup had failed; Yeltsin's had succeeded. Gorbachev was delivered to Moscow nominally as the president of a state that no longer existed, but in essence as a hostage of the White House.

The Communist papers were shut down and the Communist Party buildings were sealed up (at one and the same time they sealed up the premises of those organizations that had supported the committee, including even the Soviet of Veterans). After a few days, Gorbachev solemnly announced his departure from the Communist Party, the confiscation of its property and the dissolution of the Central Committee of the party. A new life was starting for Russia; a life without Communists, but with Yeltsin and Rutskoi.

Two questions remain to be answered: first, what was the point of the venture? And second, what do we now have as a result of its failure?

10

Winter of Discontent

In the early days after 19 August the Communist Party was swept from the scene, and a new era in the history of Russia and the world was initiated as the former Soviet Union itself gradually fell apart. The three days during which the streets were patrolled by tanks whose gun-barrels were still fitted with their covers, while the 'putschist' television informed the public in detail of the latest decrees of the 'oppositionist' Yeltsin, were the culmination of the absurdity that had already reigned in the country for several years.

In essence the coup of 19 August went ahead successfully, though this had nothing to do with the State Committee for the State of Emergency. Yeltsin and his team seized control of the Union structures, triggering successive declarations of independence and effectively pro-voking the break-up of the Soviet federation. The constitutions of the Soviet Union and of Russia became a dead letter. Yeltsin issued a stream of decrees winding up the old order. This coup ended in complete triumph.

The events of 19–21 August fulfilled much the same function as the burning of the Reichstag in Germany in 1933. In the words of the well-known philosopher Dmitri Furman, the make-believe putsch

> made it possible to destroy the opposition completely, while the 'heroic defence of the White House' provided a sort of expiation for any sins committed in the process. Once again newspapers are being shut down, though now they are the non-democratic ones. Local leaders who are considered disloyal are being removed. Russia is acting as the 'superpower' of the Union, and immediately after proclaiming the principle of the immutability of national borders, declares that it has claims to the territory of all its neighbours. In the Russian parliament, a new but at the same time age-old spirit of 'applause, rising into an ovation' reigns triumphant. The democrats are turning into 'so-called democrats' at precisely the moment

when no one is prepared any longer to describe them in this way. The victory of democracy is turning into a serious threat to democracy, and the prospect is already emerging of an authoritarian populist regime led by a 'people's president', based on a 'democratic movement' devoted to this individual, and possessing an ideology and symbolism dominated by anti-communism. Russian nationalism and religious orthodoxy in nationalist garb.[1]

A witch-hunt took place throughout the country. The epidemic of denunciations reached such a fever-pitch that even official circles became alarmed. *Rossiskaya Gazeta* observed:

> At first, it seemed that this was simply the intoxication of the first days after the victory. Now two weeks have passed, and in many quarters the passion for the hunt has not weakened; these people are zealous to expose everyone who in the days of the recent coup acted in one fashion rather than another. Someone didn't go to the barricades, but to the bread-shop. They didn't linger for a respectable half-hour in front of the leaflets pasted up in the metro, but merely slowed their steps. Then they sat for a whole day in an office where the decrees of the State Committee for the State of Emergency were being broadcast at full volume. . . . People have become frightened of their neighbours and relatives. There are odious gatherings in the work collectives: what was everyone doing during the days of the coup? At all levels, wretched superiors cringe before the 'righteous' anger of subordinates. . . . This is the reality today.[2]

There has been nothing like this in our country since the time of Stalin.

The first wave of euphoria inspired by the victory of democracy, by the liberation from totalitarianism and communism, was over. Life fell back into its usual rut. Thieves resumed thieving, bribe-takers taking bribes, politicians privatizing property, and property-owners paying protection money to racketeers.

The new authorities no longer confined themselves to mouthing slogans and making promises. They began to act, and their actions provided cause for alarm. It is not just that opposition newspapers were shut down and the CPSU dissolved. Yeltsin's Decree No. 96 abolished all the important rights of the Moscow Soviet, also effectively throwing out the law on local self-management that had been adopted by the Russian parliament. The country was ruled by decree. No one considered they needed the division of powers, and the executive power simply took over the functions of the legislative arm. The Russian parliament appeared doomed sooner or later to share the fate of the local soviets. Some publications were shut down twice over. For example, the journal *Dialog* was banned on 19 August by the State Committee for the State of Emergency, and some days later was again shut down by the Yeltsin regime. Subsequently, almost all of the newspapers that were shut down resumed publication, but with new proprietors and editors, and often with a new political orientation.

Articles appeared in the liberal newspapers which spoke boldly and honestly about the undemocratic behaviour of the democrats, about the formation of a new dictatorship, and about the threat to the freedom of the press. Unfortunately, it was too late. The new structures of authoritarian power had already been consolidated, and there was no point in people deceiving themselves, warning one another that a dictatorship was on the way. It had already arrived.

The time for protests had been several months earlier. But at that time the only people in the whole of the democratic camp who had spoken out openly against Yeltsin had been the Socialists and a few left radical groups, who had immediately been accused of complicity with the Communists. We can certainly remember how the doors of the editorial offices were shut in our faces, how the democratic press united in boycotting the information we provided – all in the name of 'democratic solidarity', which we were supposed to have violated by criticizing Gavriil Popov and Boris Yeltsin.

However, it was precisely then that the structures of the regime were being set in place. At that time, in 1990, something could still have been done – if, that is, the democratic press and intelligentsia had shown a greater willingness to swim against the current, if they had understood that dissidents were indispensable in their own ranks as well, and if they had appreciated that it is precisely the people who march out of step who defend freedom.

Our intelligentsia bears a huge, tragic responsibility. It did a great deal to expedite the formation of a new authoritarian-populist regime, and to ensure that the new masters of the country could trample as they wished on the first shoots of freedom which were only just beginning to sprout. In its time the left-wing intelligentsia in Russia and Eastern Europe, believing in socialism and even aware of the vices of Bolshevism, gave support to the Bolsheviks in the belief that their ideas represented a variant of socialist ideology. Cheerfully swelling the ranks of the 'fellow travellers', the intellectuals worked conscientiously to establish a totalitarian regime, firmly convinced that in the final analysis they were working in the interests of universal freedom. We all know what happened to the 'fellow travellers' when the regime ceased to need either intellectual apologists or their illusions and ideals. The same thing is happening today. I have no wish to serve as a prophet in this regard, but the fate of today's intelligentsia will most likely be the same.

The liberal intelligentsia of former decades had such a hatred for autocracy, and so detested fascism, that it was prepared (though with waverings and reservations) to choose communism. Today its hatred for communism has driven it to the opposite extreme.

Nezavisimaya Gazeta may still allow itself to print articles criticizing the new authorities. Arguments still rage in the soviets, and members of the Socialist Party can still speak openly of their opposition to the new regime. But this does not change the essence of the matter. The people who disagree with the government have no chance of influencing the course of events, and the state of affairs is already much worse than in the final years of the hated Communists. In the initial period the dictatorship was still able to coexist with an independent press and opposition groups. After the October Revolution, similarly non-communist parties operated relatively freely for a time, and were able to publish newspapers. In fascist Italy the Socialists at first even continued to sit in parliament, though their parliamentary leader, Mateotti, was murdered for making unacceptable radical speeches. The people who supported the new regime were not necessarily careerists or nationalists. Many of them sincerely believed that they were helping to lead the country to prosperity and democracy. Many of the Bolshevik leaders believed just as sincerely that their policies would bring happiness to the majority of the people, and that the restrictions on freedom to which the regime resorted were temporary and partial. Unfortunately, none of this prevented the consolidation of dictatorship.

One more point needs to be made, perhaps the most important of all. Disappointed with communism, and at the same time with socialism as well, the intellectuals and press commentators have become devout converts to capitalism. Observing that under communism there is neither private property nor a free market, they quite reasonably concluded that once private property and a free market were created, there would no longer be communism. And they were quite correct. The only trouble is that fascism, authoritarian populism and military dictatorship all get along fine with the market economy and private enterprise. Moreover, a young and dynamic authoritarian regime is capable of shedding a great deal more blood than a decrepit and decaying totalitarianism of the Brezhnev type.

Politics and economics are intimately connected. The press commentators were well aware of this when they were calling down thunder and lightning on the 'command-administrative system'. But for some reason they forgot about it as soon as the talk shifted to building the 'shining capitalist future'. One does not have to be a prophet to see that broad and comprehensive privatization will lead not only and not primarily to the creation of a market – so far, it has tended to create a new system of private-state monopolies – but to the creation of a class of new property-owners, drawn mainly from the ranks of the old nomenklatura but also in many cases from the criminal underworld. Against a background of general crisis and of the impoverishment of the population these people will not feel secure until a strong government, capable simply of ignoring the mood of the majority, is on hand to defend them. These new ruling strata will need not democracy, but an efficient police force.

The parties which have triumphantly proclaimed their simultaneous commitment to social guarantees and to free enterprise have neglected to mention that in the absence of the appropriate economic and financial institutions all their arguments about social justice are mere words. The institutions that ensured the social welfare of the population in the past, however bureaucratically and with typical Russian inefficiency, are now being destroyed. The inevitable response to such economic policies is social discontent, and the only way to persist with these policies despite the growing discontent is through dictatorship.

Our progressive, eminently democratic press commentators were therefore among the first to speak of the firm hand, stressing the advantages of an enlightened authoritarianism (this was in Russia!) and the need for a dictatorship along the lines of the Pinochet regime in Chile. The thousands of victims of the 'Chilean experiment' who disappeared without trace were considered to represent an acceptable price for the successes that were obtained. The point was not simply the number of victims; the main Moscow stadium (which still, it seems, bears the name of Lenin) has room for many more prisoners than that in Santiago de Chile. The real question was one of principle. How many thousands of victims were we to consider 'acceptable'? A million deaths would be appalling, but is one murder not appalling? Have we really forgotten everything we learnt from classical Russian literature, which maintained that universal happiness could not be purchased if the price were even so much as the tears of a single child?

When tanks were driving through the streets, the intellectuals took fright. Many of them also fell to thinking. It was true that the tanks were not 'their own', and the dictatorship that was in prospect was not the one they had been calling for. Many people imagined that if you fastened tricolour flags to the tanks, everything would be all right. But a tank is still a tank. We are destined to see more such machines on our streets, perhaps quite often.

We cannot remake the past, but we can understand the responsibility we bear. Today our intellectuals need above all to acknowledge their share of the blame. It would be sad if even their repentance were to come too late. It would be futile to condemn the populists for manipulating the masses and pretend that the intelligentsia was not involved, that it did not manipulate people and that it was not manipulated itself.

Repentance formed the starting point of the anti-Stalinist democratic opposition in the 1950s and 1960s. People were ashamed of what they had done or omitted to do. Once the intelligentsia's sense of shame had been transmitted to the people as a whole, communism in this country became impossible. But now we are faced with a different threat. And unfortunately, once again many of have have cause to be ashamed of ourselves.

This is only a moral response to the looming political catastrophe but it can give us the strength for political action. We cannot redress what has already been done, and we cannot return to 1989 or 1990. But we can work for the future. This means trying to establish a strong political left, in the European sense of the word; it means building a strong organization acting as an opposition to the new regime. Opposition is required not only to the regime's anti-democratic 'excesses', but also to its economic policies. This means that it is essential to resist the process of bureaucratic privatization, and to defend, transform and democratize the social sector without which there cannot be a 'mixed economy'. It also means defending the local soviets, not only as organs of power but also as owners of property, as structures ensuring a balanced social and economic development.

The bare left flank of our political anatomy constitutes a wound through which life is ebbing from our already weakened civil society. The new regime needs an effective opposition now, while the government is still popular and, as a result, not yet profoundly repressive. Otherwise, it will soon become impossible to form any kind of legal opposition.

The collapse of the CPSU has posed the question of what formations will take its place. The property of the Communist Party has already been expropriated, but who is to inherit the section of the CPSU membership that wishes to remain politically active? One claimant to this inheritance is the party set up by Colonel Rutskoi; known originally as the Democratic Party of Communists of Russia (DPKR), this grouping hurriedly changed its name after the events of 21 August 1991 and became the Party of Free Russia (PSR). With its more rigid party structure, disciplined cadres and strong leader, this party is envisaged as the core of the new mass popular organization into which the Democratic Russia Movement (DDR) is supposed to evolve. Although conflicts and power struggles are possible between the activists of the DDR and the PSR, on the whole they are pursuing the same orientation, and have already defined specific roles for themselves. Both organizations are closely linked to the new Russian authorities and in essence have inherited the functions of the CPSU as the ruling party.

After the events of 19 to 21 August 1991 Rutskoi's position was strengthened dramatically. The Party of Free Russia defined itself as an organization oriented above all towards nationalist concepts. Nothing remained of communism even in the party's name. The PSR promised workers that their social guarantees would be defended, but no one was prepared to say how this would be achieved in practice.

The exit of the CPSU from the political scene created a paradoxical situation. On the one hand large numbers of people disowned communism and socialism, while on the other hand there are millions of people, often quite active politically, who still hold to these ideas but who could not find an organization through which to express their beliefs. The ruling bloc, which is oriented towards the traditional ideals of Western right-wingers (property, order and national honour), lacks a serious opponent expressing the values of the European left (the right to work, participation in management, internationalism and so forth). The new monopoly of political power carries within it the seed of a right-wing dictatorship. Dissatisfaction with the policies of the new leaders may come to be expressed in spontaneous revolts and wildcat strikes, which in turn may be used as a pretext for further 'turns of the screw'.

On the left there is now a vacuum. For good or ill, the CPSU sought up to a certain point to play the role of an opposition party, oriented towards left-wing values. The Communist Party leadership played this role extremely badly, since its attempts were hindered by its entire previous experience, by the party's anti-democratic structure and, most importantly, by the interests of the party nomenklatura itself, since this group had no links whatever with the workers. With the collapse of the CPSU the left flank of our social body was stripped naked. But then the possibility appeared of forming a new, powerful, modern and democratic left organization, which would not carry the burden of responsibility for the CPSU's Stalinist past, and which would have a totally different structure.

Attempts are being made to establish a new left party on the basis of the fragments of the CPSU, but it is already clear that these efforts are doomed to failure. Gorbachev's move to form his own party attracted no support outside the former apparatus of the CPSU Central Committee. A similar initiative by Oleg Witte in Leningrad and Otto Latsis in

Moscow also failed for lack of new ideas and members. Following these unsuccessful attempts to found an organization, both Witte and Latsis forswore active political involvement and applied themselves to journalism. In November and December 1991 an Organizing Committee for a Socialist Workers' Party was announced by Roy Medvedev and some other former members of the CPSU. According to its first declaration this group aimed to become a loyal opposition to Yeltsin, an ambition which could easily founder on the fact that Yeltsin does not want an opposition of any description.

The hide-bound Stalinists were more successful due to their simple slogans and clearly formulated demands, but they were condemned to work in conditions of semi-legality, and by no stretch of the imagination could they be called a democratic or progressive force.

In August 1991 the persecutors and the persecuted finally changed places. The old Communist Party was outlawed, and the few activists who remained true to its banner assembled around positions of orthodox, uncompromising Bolshevism. A new communist movement was arising, one that was quite unlike Gorbachev's CPSU with its diverse fractions and groups. The new movement was vital, determined and more or less homogeneous.

The sources of the Communists' strength were always much broader than their simple, easily understood slogans. The Communist organizations possessed a key advantage in that they appealed to completely valid workers' interests and pointed to real problems and vices of the capitalist system. After seventy-three years of Communist rule, people who were accustomed to totally different problems and quite different forms of alienation and exploitation were naturally inclined to think that everything the CPSU propagandists had said was fiction and demagogy. But once these people actually came face to face with the new situation, they found that the vices of capitalism were absolutely real. This inevitably increased the authority of those Communists who remained true to their colours.

The tragedy of the Communist movement or, to be more precise, the tragedy of the masses who supported these groups, lay in the fact that while pointing to real social maladies the Communist parties suggested cures that were worse than the disease. But until other, more effective and democratic medicines appeared, the Communist organizations would remain attractive to the masses.

In Russia people love the persecuted and hate the persecutors. They loved Yeltsin so long as he was a victim. Now they have begun to love and pity Yeltsin's victims, a trend likely to become much more pronounced, given the already disturbing degree of persecution of dissident thinkers. Elena Bonner, the widow of Andrei Sakharov, has spoken of the worrying violation of individual rights by the new Russian authorities. The regime might succeed in stabilizing itself through repression and a monopoly on propaganda. But the invariable lesson of history is that in driving its opponents underground it digs its own grave.

But who will bury Yeltsinism? In the legal struggle, in elections and in theoretical debates, the democratic left – that is, the Socialists and the new Party of Labour – has an enormous advantage over the neo-Bolsheviks. But under conditions in which the left is subject to persecution, the Communists with their paramilitary discipline will gain in strength. Alexander Rutskoi has openly attacked Yeltsin for instability and recklessness. Even Zhirinovsky, with his nationalist demagogy and clownish antics, exploits popular discontent.

It was appropriate that at its Second Congress the Socialist Party began to speak of a new politics oriented to the needs of the mass of people, a politics just as clearly opposed to the government of Gorbachev and Pavlov as it was to the anti-communist oppositionists who refused to take the needs of the majority into account. The choice which the Socialists placed before society might have been summed up as follows: 'Either us, or Polozkov.' Today Polozkov and his Russian Communist Party have vanished from the scene, but they have many heirs in such illegal or semi-legal organizations as the United Front of Workers, the new Communist parties, and the Communist Initiative movement.

Like the Socialists, these groups are trying to address a population that has grown tired of the squabbling of professional politicians, and which dreams of the restoration of stability and social guarantees. Of today's left-wing opposition forces, some call for a return to the past, for restoring the peaceful times of 'stagnation', which not even Polozkov has the power to bring back. Others speak of a democracy that corresponds to our realities and needs.

The rise of a strong and influential left party, acting in opposition to the new regime, would not only represent a way out of the ideological impasse. It would also be the sole guarantee that the clash of irresponsible political groups would not lead the country into economic chaos and a new dictatorship. Democracy comes into being where the interests of the masses rate higher than the interests of the leaders, and where the question of sovereignty does not prevent ways being found to ensure the social protection of the population. Democracy begins with respect for the concrete interests of the majority, and only policies aimed at defending these interests can bring society the stability for which so many people long.

The Party of Labour has turned out to be the only serious attempt to counterpose a left alternative to the emerging Yeltsin dictatorship. On 31 September *Moskovskaya Pravda*, followed later by the Moscow trade union newspaper *Solidarnost*, published an appeal by the organizers of the Party of Labour stating that the new body 'had to become a party of political support for the trade unions and the workers' movement'.[3] To the anti-communism, anti-socialism and nationalism of the new authorities, the appeal counterposed the principles of democratic participation by workers in management, along with traditional socialist values. However, the call was not for the founding of an ideological tendency, but for the building of an organization reflecting concrete interests. The trade unions cannot and must not identify themselves with the Party of Labour, but it is also clear that one cannot talk of a mass left party expressing the interests of the workers if this party does not have support within the trade union organizations.

The plans for the Party of Labour include the possibility of a relatively broad pluralism, allowing the organization to attract people from various currents ranging from left social democrats and socialists to democratic communists. These people will be united not around ideological dogmas, but upon the social base they have in common. While the party will attract former Communists, it will not be a successor to the CPSU, and will bear no responsibility for that organization's past. There is now no need, at least for left socialists, to explain how they differ from the CPSU and to make excuses for actions which they never committed. Now that the threat to human rights stems not from those who used to promise the shining communist future, but from those who tell the people fairy stories about steady progress to general prosperity under an orthodox people's capitalism, socialists have a much better chance of making themselves understood.

With Yeltsin at the helm the prospects for making a reality of the new Commonwealth seem remote. The Ukraine voted for independence in December 1991. The Russian president at last tired of Gorbachev presenting himself to the world as the president of a state that did not exist, informing him that he must vacate the Kremlin by the end of the year. The Soviet flag was lowered and the Russian flag was raised – meagre symbolic satisfaction for the devastating blow of draconian price rises which ushered in the New Year. Meanwhile in Georgia the president, elected in May 1991 with over 80 per cent of the votes, was surrounded in the parliament and driven into exile by a rival gang of 'democrats'. Following the shooting of two participants in a demonstration in support of the ousted president, Shevardnadze, the liberal so beloved of the Western media and the Western political establishment, called for strict measures to restore order. As the former Communist boss in Georgia, Shevardnadze certainly knew how to apply strict measures in that republic. Such events have ominous implications for the rest of the ex-USSR. *Kommersant*'s comment that we are passing through a brief Weimar period was apparently borne out as Minsk – a fair Soviet equivalent to Weimar – was chosen as the place to launch the flimsy new 'Commonwealth of Independent States'. But in truth our situation is different from that of Weimar because of the extreme weakness of our political institutions and parties. Weimar lasted for over a decade whereas our new order is already teetering on the brink.

A historical catastrophe has already occurred, though not everyone yet understands this. While the old order has been pronounced dead viable new structures have not appeared. What claims to be new is burdened by personnel, habits and a programme elaborated precisely by that old Soviet order in which nobody believes. The various ex-Soviet republics retain not only their Soviet form but, in most cases, also a leadership which derives from the old Union. The Soviet empire has fallen apart as did those of Alexander and Charlemagne with the local republican chiefs declaring their own principalities and satrapies. A Commonwealth of Independent States has been proclaimed but with such haste and imprecision that no one really knows to whom the assets and apparatus of the former Union belong. Indeed the sudden appearance of fifteen brand new 'independent states' has about it something of a bureaucratic conjuring trick. While new republican governments undoubtedly exist, exercising far more authority than before, so do the former armed forces and much of the military-industrial complex.

In Russia and elsewhere the new apparatus itself is intimately linked to the emergence of new social forces, notably the middle classes. Of course there has been a large-scale reshuffling of the bureaucratic pack and some modest pruning; by the end of December 1991 some sixty thousand former Soviet officials were said to be unemployed, but the majority were re-employed by the Russian republic. If economic catastrophes destroy the remaining popular belief in these new authorities, then the military-industrial complex will search for a new solution, one which is likely to be no less wasteful and destructive than that so recklessly undertaken by Yeltsin. Still, the former Soviet lands can look forward to the future; there will be life after the catastrophe. In Russia we intend to survive and try to build a normal human existence.

The end of the Communist era has not meant the triumph of democracy. But it has marked the beginning of a new stage in the development of society, when once again, just as in Russia at the end of the last century, the struggle for socialist ideas is becoming inseparable from the struggle for freedom. We have come full circle. We can only hope that history has at last taught us something. At least we are now elaborating an alternative based on the real problems of our people.

What Next?

The main argument advanced by the post-Communist governments in Poland has been that there is no alternative. Even if the chosen path leads to an impasse, the argument runs, there can be no other course. But there is an alternative. To understand what it is, one has to change one's point of reference and look at the situation not from the offices of the nomenklatura or the parliamentary rostrums, but from the position of the old and new privileged groups, and from the point of view of the majority of the population who have nothing to live on but their wages. Finally, one must recognize that the market does not solve the problems, but only establishes certain not wholly rational rules.

The new situation has radically altered the relationship of political forces. Earlier, it was still possible to draw distinctions on the basis of 'they' (the conservatives) and 'we' (the democrats), and to confine oneself to simple slogans such as 'Yes to changes!' or 'Long live multi-party pluralism!' Today everyone says they support multi-party pluralism though we actually have no real parties. The old Communist Party apparatus has broken into a thousand pieces. Some are now liberals, some have grabbed chunks of former state property, some are hoping to receive a pension and wondering what it will buy. At the lower levels a few are even committed to building trade unions.

The most important criterion has become not the relationship to the old bureaucracy – which has crumbled – but the relationship of the various players to the liberal programme of raising prices, abandoning all social guarantees and privatizing assets. A situation has arisen in which it is essential, in the name of democracy and the people's living standards, to oppose the reforms. The words 'left' and 'right', which are used in the Soviet Union in a totally confused way, are beginning to regain their original European meanings. The leftists are those who make their first priority the defence of workers' interests; the rightists are those who defend the interests of the property-owners and the power of the possessing groups. The leftists are those for whom progress in unthinkable without democracy; the rightists, those who argue that democracy and social rights may be sacrificed in the name of progress.

The left alternative presupposes that it is essential to conduct a conscious and deliberate policy of modernization under the control of democratic institutions. Scientific establishments must be radically transformed, and a modern infrastructure created. What we should be doing is not simply adopting anti-monopoly laws, but carrying out a long and serious process of demonopolization. We should not just be protecting the environment, but implementing a programme of ecologizing the economy, introducing greener technology and developing new patterns of consumption. We should not just be demanding higher efficiency from enterprises, but creating favourable circumstances for their rapid technological renewal through guaranteeing them access to cheap modern technologies. We should be expediting the retraining of workers, and creating new jobs in priority areas.

The country's development can create opportunities for the formation and growth of a modern private sector, but under present conditions in the ex-USSR private enterprise does not have the potential to ensure rapid and effective modernization while simultaneously broadening and maintaining social guarantees. In current circumstances it will be unable to guarantee people better working conditions, let alone grant them the right to participate in decision-making, or overcome the alienation of the worker from the means of production.

The labour collectives, which today are aiming to become the owners of their enterprises, have already purchased the factories many times over through their labour. But the simple transfer of enterprises into the indivisible collective property of the workers, and the formation of democratic organs allowing the collectives to participate in decision-making, will not in itself solve the problems of modernization.

If the self-managed enterprises are simply handed over to their labour collectives and left to the mercy of fate, then with their obsolete equipment, uncompetitive production, 'dirty' technologies and lack of managerial culture, they will hardly be able to stand on their own feet. For socialists, self-management or the participation of workers in decision-making is an indispensable element of democracy, which must not stop at the factory gates. But democracy in production cannot take the place of an economic strategy.

Successful modernization is inconceivable without concentrated state investment in priority areas. We need to build roads, to encourage the modernization of production and, not least, its ecologization. We need an economy which allows us to produce more while polluting less and consuming fewer resources. We need to form local production organizations which use resources available locally and which provide work for people near their homes. All this is simply inconceivable without national, regional and local development programmes, relying on the socialized sector.

Such an economic policy can be implemented using social investment funds at various levels. It presupposes the existence of a central planning system responsible to the elected parliament for establishing national development projects. It also presupposes the ability of the state to exercise flexible control over the prices of basic goods, encouraging the introduction of ecologically clean, resource-saving technologies.

Today we regard any broadening of the economic role of the state as undesirable, since the existing state is hostile to us. The state represents the interests of the bureaucracy, and if the reforms are successful, the state will ensure that the oligarchy's newly acquired property is defended. We therefore need to 'replace the state'. This is not simply a matter of electing good democrats to replace the apparatchiks in the old soviets, but of decisively altering the whole structure of power, of establishing new institutions with direct links to the people. We need a decentralized and democratized government which also possesses full authority, is socially responsible, and is under the control of the people. In other words, 'the basic question of every revolution' – the question of power – has to be solved.

Naturally, such questions do not solve themselves. Nothing will change until political forces arise which are capable of struggling for the creation of a new state. The Socialist initiative of June 1990 and the negotiations to form a Party of Labour in the closing months of 1991 and early months of 1992 were important steps on the road to forming a left alternative. So long as Socialists remain an insignificant minority in the soviets, one can hardly speak of a new political force having arisen. But the changing situation is creating an objective need for a mass left movement. The alternative to liberal reforms can only be revolutionary reforms, of the kind which the left currents and pro-Party of Labour groups are demanding. The overall programme of the left bloc can be set out as follows:

1. Market relations are indispensable, but they should not become the basic regulator of social and economic life. The market can act as a controlling mechanism feeding back information about the economy,

but its influence should not be allowed to extend beyond the economic sphere.

2. It is essential to establish an integral system of self-management and democratic planning capable of ensuring that the workers and all other citizens will be able to take part in making decisions that affect them, and that a democratic mechanism exists for the reconciliation of conflicting interests. The development of the market must have a place within the framework of this democratic planning.

3. It is essential to establish a general mechanism for ensuring social guarantees, replacing bureaucratic handouts with inalienable, legally guaranteed citizens' rights. Education, health care and housing must be available to all.

4. Political democracy is the supreme value. In cases where the interests of a particular social group or party conflict with the development of democracy, preference must be given to democracy. If economic projects do not enjoy the support of the majority they should not go ahead. The combination of economic and political democracy will create conditions in which all the participants in political struggles and all interest groups will be forced to consider the interests of other strata and to try to come up with strategies acceptable to the majority.

5. Where the principle of the 'rights of nations' conflicts with the principles of human rights, preference must be given to human rights. The right of nations to self-determination and national renewal must not be realized at the expense of denying minorities their rights or of breaching democratic norms.

Leftists oppose turning state enterprises into private companies or joint-stock firms (which in essence amount to the same thing). The present form of state property is clearly unable to solve the problems facing our society and has nothing in common with socialism; such state firms also existed in Tsarist Russia. The state has owned a large part of the economy and planned it in a centralized fashion as far back in history as ancient China and Egypt. Democratic changes are impossible unless this state property is transformed into social property. In place of the old ministries and new bureaucratic monopolies, associations of self-managed enterprises can be established, and a significant part of the economy can be placed under the control of municipal bodies. Finally, appropriate conditions must be created for the rise of genuine co-operatives – free associations of workers, holding the means of production in common and oriented towards the satisfaction of social needs.

A profound reform of the entire system of government, carried out on a popular basis, will inevitably challenge Russia's new bureaucratic structures. Such a reform will not work without free elections, independent trade unions and democratically chosen organs of productive self-management and soviets at all levels. These democratic structures are vitally necessary for ensuring a new system of decision-making. It is precisely for this reason that the 'left model' gives priority to realizing the greatest possible political freedom for the people, something which is in no way essential for carrying out the 'liberal' reforms.

The new situation demands a new opposition: society must be defended from reformers who pursue what are in essence profoundly conservative goals. An alternative will arise as soon as people begin to struggle for it.

The future will show whether the socialists, who today are a comparatively small social current, will be able to combine into a genuine political force, and whether the workers' movement will follow behind them (or march with them). But one thing is already clear: what society needs most is not an increase in the number of parties, but the formation of real alternatives reflecting the interests of the various social strata.

In the final analysis, the programme of 'market Stalinism' in its various guises is strikingly reminiscent of the ideas of right-wing liberal or 'neoconservative' politicians in the West and the Third World. On the other hand the ideology of the socialist left in the former Eastern bloc coincides in its main outlines with the conceptions of Western leftists. Naturally, the degree of radicalism might be different, and also the circumstances, but the common ground in terms of values is obvious. It is no accident that Western rightists applaud the 'bold liberal reforms' in the former Communist countries while the leftists are making contact with the growing socialist and self-management movements. Western society, like our own, is going through a period of change. And the choice in the Soviet Union is analogous: either private reforms for the elite, with the acquiescence of the masses ensured by the use of the 'firm hand', or democracy for all. But in Soviet conditions, in the complete absence of real democratic conditions or institutions, the stakes and the dangers are much higher. If market Stalinism is implemented with the consistency it requires, it could turn out to be many times more cruel than Thatcherism in Britain.

For several years liberal ideologues have argued that the transition to capitalism will mean the transformation of Russia and Eastern Europe into 'normal' societies. And it is true that a totalitarian society can hardly be called 'normal'. Is it at all normal for the exploitation and oppression of workers to be masked by talk of 'socialism', and for armed intervention in the affairs of independent states to be termed fraternal international aid? Is it really normal that the provision of social guarantees should also signify the total dependence of the workers on state functionaries?

The fact is that the liberal heirs of totalitarianism really are transforming Russia and Eastern Europe into part of the 'normal world'. While introducing the capitalist market, the liberals are at the same time forcing the people to try to cope with all the problems encountered by the majority of workers in the 'normal' capitalist world: unemployment, poverty and the absence of civil freedoms.

Meanwhile a new situation, which in its way is more normal, is beginning to emerge. In the final analysis socialism is nothing other than the democratic alternative to capitalism. In earlier times, before people had encountered real capitalism, it was difficult for socialists in the former Eastern bloc to explain to people who had been cut off from the real world by propaganda why it was that the market would not lead automatically to prosperity, and why bourgeois social relations do not in the least act as guarantees of political rights. Now we are about to grasp all this on the basis of our own experience.

The great virtue of the market lies in the fact that it helps workers to understand their own interests better. Previously, each of us confronted a faceless state. Now we are exploited by oligarchs who have resolved to act openly as property-owners. The roles have taken on their proper form, and it is becoming harder all the time to confuse and deceive the people. Naturally, the oligarchs are no more willing to surrender their power under the new conditions than under the old, and are quite willing to resort to repression. But the old 'monolithic' totalitarianism has gone for good. People who have experienced totalitarianism have no wish to revert to the status of mindless drudges, even if they do not as yet understand how to free themselves.

The new conditions are forcing the workers to organize themselves. As we come to recognize our own interests, we will learn to defend them. The need is emerging for a strong left movement, which will figure more and more as part of the international forces of the left. As we join the 'normal' world, we are learning to ask 'normal' questions. We are beginning to understand that, just as Stalin's 'communism' was not the only form of slavery, 'Western democracy' is not the sole possible form of freedom; that in the 'normal world' developed and democratic capitalism is a luxury for the elite, one which for us is completely inaccessible. This is forcing us to seek our own new paths, and to make a choice. The choice we make will determine where we stand in our country's political life, on the left or on the right.

Notes

1. *Nezavisimaya Gazeta*, 3 September 1991.
2. *Rossiskaya Gazeta*, 5 September 1991.

11

Russia on the Brink of New Battles

The removal from power of Soviet President Gorbachev by the Russian government – de facto in the last days of August 1991 and then formally at the end of December – did not provoke any protests, despite the fact that the intention of former Soviet prime minister Pavlov and vice-president Yanayev to edge him out (most probably temporarily) and take his place qualified as treason. No one felt sorry for Gorbachev, who in the minds of the people was associated with the failures of the previous five years, but the collapse of the president's power automatically entailed the liquidation of the Union as well. The feudal structure of power that had arisen and consolidated itself unavoidably linked the fate of the state institutions with the future of the ruler.[1] If Russia was to turn into Yeltsin's 'domain', then the centre had become Gorbachev's personal property, and the triumph of the former over the latter in their personal rivalry could only be accompanied by the dissolution of the centre as such.

The collapse of the Union provoked a new wave of interethnic conflicts, and political and economic instability. The triumph of August was expressed in the dissolution of the CPSU and an orgy of appropriation of party property by the new authorities and their hangers-on. Communist newspapers were closed and then allowed to reopen, but in conditions that left them vulnerable to pressure, both political and commercial. The leading representatives of the CPSU in the Congress of People's Deputies tamely assented to these measures, only putting up a struggle when the prospect arose of their salaries being stopped forthwith.

The CPSU was not the only casualty of the August events. The Russian government blatantly flouted its own promises and democratic laws. The freely elected local soviets were deprived of power and their authority was transferred to representatives of the president. By the end of the year, representative and judicial organs had largely lost the struggle to control the executive power. The Russian Federation's

Congress of People's Deputies (which, in any case, meets infrequently) was deprived in the autumn of the power to call cabinet ministers to account. Yeltsin himself assumed the posts of president, prime minister and defence minister. The foundation of a 'strong executive power' was only the first step on the road to the reforms promised by the government, and was designed to ensure the triumph of capitalism in Russia in the shortest possible time. Periodically, the Congress has sought to retrieve powers from Yeltsin and make the government directly accountable. But the president has been able, time and time again, to call the bluff of his parliamentary critics; they have no real alternative to his programme, and many of them, as hangovers from the old order, lack political credibility. Yeltsin's administration, lacking coherence in policy-making and with no clear long-term goals, is travelling erratically down the wrong road. The government takes one muddle-headed and ill-considered decision after another; it is obvious to anyone who manages to read Yeltsin's decrees that they contradict each other, the existing laws and international norms. Indeed, Yeltsin's arbitrary use of power has alarmed even those like Anatoly Sobchak, the mayor of St Petersburg, who otherwise endorse the neoliberal line. Yet this only affords a hint of the political incoherence and economic folly that characterizes the regime. The government has driven defiantly over the potholes of the crisis, doggedly sticking to its twists and turns, promising us every day that it is just on the point of taking us on to the 'highway of world civilization' which, it is claimed, leads to the 'common European home'. It is hard to credit that the powers-that-be could really believe in all this nonsense, but, judging by their actions, they have learned to deceive themselves more effectively than they have been able to pull the wool over the eyes of the public. Many of the phrases used to justify the new programmes have been simply warmed-up versions of the old perestroika and 'five hundred days' of transition to the free market.

Confidence in the president and his team suffered as winter set in and the promised radical economic reforms were unveiled. The authorities reacted in reflex fashion to the people's increasing lack of trust by reinforcing their propaganda campaign and reshuffling the higher echelons of the administration. But the citizens of Russia had been fed such a surfeit of demagogic promises and propagandist myths during the years of perestroika, and were so tired of the fleeting glimpses of political figures on television, that such measures only intensified the crisis of confidence.

Gaidar's Road to Ruin

Yeltsin and his entourage placed their hopes in the rapid development of the reform programme proposed by Yegor Gaidar, a former associate editor of *Kommunist* and department editor of *Pravda*, who was immediately dubbed the 'Russian Balcerowicz'. If the 'Balcerowicz Plan' in Poland had, at the cost of a catastrophic drop in the already low living standards and a slump in production, permitted the temporary stabilization of the national currency, guaranteed the convertibility of the zloty, and reinforced the position of the new class of big proprietors (who had to a significant degree emerged from among the ranks of the old party bureaucracy), then Gaidar's plan set itself the same goals in conditions where the slump in production had already reached menacing proportions. Unlike in Poland, where the 'Balcerowicz Plan' initially enjoyed the support of the population, in Russia Gaidar's proposals found no comprehension even in the government. Representatives of the military-industrial complex were unable to reach an understanding with those defending the interests of speculators, and the leaders of the various bureaucratic clans could find no grounds for accord on the proposed privatization plans. These squabbles at the top soon became known to the wider public. During a trip to Siberia, Vice-President Alexander Rutskoi, leader of the Party of Free Russia, openly attacked Gaidar's government, calling him and his colleagues 'boys in pink knickerbockers',[2] an appellation repeated by all newspapers without exception. (Even though a majority of the press condemned Rutskoi, they still applied this nickname to Gaidar and his team.) The launching of the new plan in January 1992 led to very sharp price rises. Meanwhile, privatization of enterprises has destroyed economic links; instead of creating a market, the policies of Gaidar and Yeltsin have undermined its foundations.

Gaidar's economic failures were predetermined not only by a false understanding of the prospects of the Russian economy and a total lack of interest in the real conditions for development in the country, but by the wrong-headedness of the government's economic philosophy. On the one hand, Yegor Gaidar, like Yeltsin, was prepared to follow any recommendations made by the International Monetary Fund and by conservative Western experts, believing their pledge to turn Russia into a modern industrial power capable of competing with the West. And, on the other hand, he and his supporters still toyed with illusions concerning their own roles, unconscious of the fact that, by following such a strategy, they could, at best, play only the part of colonizers and representatives of Western interests in their own country.

In repeating the slogans of Western neoconservatism, the Russian ideologists consciously closed their eyes to the fact that its key economic concepts were elaborated, and the prescriptions applied, in conditions utterly different from those now confronting Russia. The path was a false one because no 'highway' of European (let alone world) civilization exists, and the experience of the West teaches us only that successful countries have never tried to copy existing models. The proclaimed goal of becoming a developed capitalist state in the mould of Britain or France is simply objectively unattainable. It is naïve in the extreme to think that the gulf in levels of development and wealth can be bridged with the help of a few salutary *laissez faire* prescriptions. If such were feasible, after all, poor and backward countries would have ceased to exist long ago. Meanwhile, it remains the case that the overwhelming majority of countries living under capitalism are underdeveloped. Not only are their economies poor, and their populations living in conditions of poverty, but indeed over the past two decades, despite scrupulous observation of all the rules of bourgeois society, they have become even poorer.[3]

The prescriptions of the Russian liberal ideologists bring to mind the famous book *One Hundred Ways to Get Rich*. As a rule, neither the readers nor the authors of such books become millionaires. If these individuals are so clever, one must ask, why have they not made their own fortunes?

In fact, the issue before us is not how to join the ranks of successful Western countries but, rather, how simply to survive, how to find a way out of the crisis and then regain even the level of the Brezhnevite 1970s. Alas, the present Russian government cannot provide a satisfactory answer to these questions. Instead of an anti-crisis strategy, they announce one ambitious, wholly traditional master plan after another. The government, composed of former Communist apparatchiks, has contrived to inherit many of the defects of the old Communist regime, without retaining a single one of its virtues. Russian President Boris Yeltsin, Mayor of Moscow Gavriil Popov, and the 'architect of reform' Yegor Gaidar have pledged to solve all problems by achieving the economic miracle of universal privatization; but, as has happened before in the country's history, the latest campaign is not merely failing to achieve the promised results, but is undermining an already weakened economy. The slogan of universal privatization is not just akin to total collectivization under Stalin or the general introduction of maize under Khrushchev; it has also turned out to be no less dangerous economically.[4]

In the same way as Stalin and his entourage, in undertaking collectivization, could only guess some of the possible negative consequences and were prepared to accept them for the sake of more important goals, Gaidar and Yeltsin are now prepared to liquidate a large part of Russia's economic potential in the name of the triumph of capitalism. As in the 1930s, the rulers' real goals have little to do with the development of those sectors of the economy intended for privatization/collectivization. The motivation is not to produce more, but to grab property: first, expropriate the petty producer in favour of the collective proprietor – the nomenklatura bureaucracy – then divide up state property between the various groups and figures in this bureaucracy. For the creators of such reforms, a drop in production and even hunger are no more than the acceptable 'costs of progress'.

The authorities' policies look rather less senseless if we understand that, in fact, the ruling circles are not striving to pull the country out of the crisis. They have, rather, set themselves another goal: to utilize the crisis for their own personal enrichment. And they are a long way towards achieving their aims. The liberalization of prices in January 1992 saw the cost of basic consumer goods increase to seven times their cost a year before. Some wage earners received an increase in their salaries to 'compensate', but were lucky to get a threefold increase. Hyperinflation has the effect of definitively depreciating the savings of intermediate strata and widening the gulf between those who already have power and property and those who live on wages, even if these rise in line with inflation. Students, retired people and the unemployed are even worse hit; and it is predicted that the numbers of the unemployed will run into many millions unless the present ruinous course is abandoned.

What sort of privatization can we talk about in the absence of a functioning market economy, in a country where laws do not operate; where there is no developed system of commercial law; and, most important, where there is no civilized and responsible bourgeoisie? Who intends to buy what? And how many stories have we been told about the entrepreneurial spirit that is just about to burst forth and transform the country, when we know full well that private enterprise has never and nowhere arisen on the basis of the privatization of centralized state monopolies; that the bourgeoisie needs several generations in the most favourable conditions to come into existence, and several more generation to become civilized. Whether this path is possible for Russia in the twenty-first century is a piece of pointless speculation. We simply do not have the time; the questions posed by the current crisis must be answered today, not after five generations.

The scandals and manifest corruption that accompanied the drive towards privatization resulted only in conflict between rival plans, each as untenable as the next. The deadlock will continue because the problem is insoluble: privatization cannot be implemented without monstrous abuses, due to the absence of a market and functioning laws. It is a nonsense to argue that everyone should become proprietors while simultaneously proposing the creation of a labour market – for who would then be hired to work? A market cannot be created simply by privatizing property, as the new private monopolies retain a non-market structure and a link with the state bureaucracy, and they have inherited all the flaws of the failed economic system – those very features that generated the current crisis. Finally and most important, in conditions of general uncertainty it is impossible to carry out privatization without breaking already weakened economic links and undermining managerial confidence and efficacy; and of course that means without undermining production, destroying the productive forces, increasing unemployment and thereby generally deepening the crisis.

Growing discontent has inevitably found its expression in increasing opposition to the regime, although the majority of political groupings in the country have so far proved incapable of establishing a real alternative. For his part, Vice-President Rutskoi has continued to denounce the reckless character of the reform programme. The president of the Russian People's Congress, Khasbulatov, also sought to distance himself from unpopular features of the reform. In April 1992 Yeltsin moved his key aides, Yegor Gaidar and V. Burbulis, to new posts in order to minimize the scope for parliamentary scrutiny of their activities. Nevertheless, despite the existence of widespread opposition to the Gaidar plan, few members of the political class are willing to give up the illusion of 'radical reform' leading to a rapid capitalist transformation. Right-wing parties (which in Russia include, alongside the Republicans, the Movement for Democratic Reforms, the Party of Free Russia and also the social democrats), while critical of the government, on the whole share its economic programme. As a result, their protests amount to little more than a demand for new and 'more competent' people to be appointed to leadership posts from among the ranks of their own parties. This also holds for the Liberal leader Zhirinovsky, with his demagogic and ultra-nationalist appeals. As regards the left, they have neither strong organization nor political experience, and they lack vital access to the mass media.

The Emergence of an Opposition

In these conditions a vacuum exists where there should be a strong opposition. The most visible forces opposing the government's programme have been CPSU loyalists; but they can never form the nucleus of an alternative that might win the confidence of the mass of people. It is far more likely that the force capable of filling this vacuum will turn out to be the trade unions. Under the influence of Polish Solidarity, the idea of powerful and independent trade unions has caught the imagination of the ideologists of both the socialist left and also, at times, the liberal right. However, following the collapse of the Communist systems in Eastern Europe, free trade unions based on the Polish model have everywhere found themselves in crisis. Even in Poland itself, Solidarity is already both smaller and less effective than the old unions inherited from the Jaruzelski regime. At a time when the former Communist unions are trying to reconstruct themselves and defend the interests of their members, some Solidarity figures are calling on the workers to make sacrifices in the name of democracy, while others are engaged in damaging factional struggles.

Over the course of many years, the official ('old') trade unions in Russia had a truly miserable existence. With no role as independent representatives of the waged workers, trade-union organizations were primarily occupied in the redistribution of goods in short supply and arranging holidays for workers and their families. Positions in the union apparatus were filled with second-rate party and state officials. As a result, even during the years of Gorbachev's perestroika, when a sharp political struggle raged within a majority of official bodies, the unions proved to be useless. The overall picture has remained discouraging although profound changes have taken place in the old union bodies. Following comparatively free elections, new people appeared in the leadership of trade-union organizations in Moscow, St Petersburg and a number of other major industrial centres in the course of 1990 and 1991. In St Petersburg this reorganization even led to an internal crisis: the new leadership of the city federation encountered direct sabotage on the part of middle-level union bureaucrats. Federation leaders, having gained support in the enterprises, were unable to secure the transfer of funds from the city's industrial branch unions. As a result, trade-union organizations in major factories even threatened to leave the industrial branch and join the federation as autonomous members. In Moscow there existed a quite different situation. After Mikhail Shmakov became head of the local union federation (MFTU), the organization's structure was altered and its activity stepped up. In attempting to pursue an independent line, the MFTU came into sharp conflict with the CPSU and also with the city's new 'democratic' rulers and the leadership of the Federation of Independent Trade Unions of Russia (FNPR). Articles appeared in the press denouncing the MFTU's 'conservatism' – its failure to express delight at the policy of wholesale privatization coupled with the securing of indexation of wages and retraining programmes for workers threatened by redundancy.

In early autumn 1991, through inertia, the government adopted some propagandist proposals that might have demonstrated their concern for the workers had they not been immediately belied by the announcement of swingeing imminent price rises and the ending of subsidies. With the reorganization of the Russian government, and the appointment of Yegor Gaidar as deputy prime minister responsible for the reforms, the intended course became clear, particularly as not one of the protective measures announced earlier had been implemented.

Meanwhile, the Moscow trade unions insisted that the authorities honour their promises. At first they had the support – albeit halfhearted – of the FNPR leadership. On 23 October 1991, a mass rally, organized by MFTU, took place in Manezh Square in Moscow. The authorities tried to impose a ban, but at the last moment were forced to compromise with the unions. More than forty thousand turned out for what was, essentially, the first mass action against Yeltsin's reforms. The rally had its effect. A majority of the Russian parliament approved a draft law on the indexation of workers' incomes to give a majority of the population some protection in conditions of rapidly rising prices. However, the government's unwillingness to make any new concessions was made apparent. At the end of November, prices began to rise rapidly; wages, however, remained under strict control. In response, new protests were organized by MFTU, but this time the capital's leadership refused to meet the union leaders. Pickets and union-organized rallies were declared illegal and the police received instructions to disperse them. This order was not, however, carried out, as the sympathy of the police lay with the demonstrators.

Following the transformation of the Moscow City Council of Trade Unions into the MFTU, the Moscow unions declared their political neutrality in accordance with the line promulgated by the FNPR. Nonetheless, the conflict between unions and authorities inevitably acquired political significance. Without a strong political organization, however, the workers' movement could not successfully resist the government.

A Third Force?

Efforts to resurrect the Communist Party were undertaken immediately after the August events but without real hope of success. The self-liquidation of the CPSU's leading bodies guaranteed that any group of party members proclaiming itself the rightful heir would have equal rights with any other such grouping. Not surprisingly, the result was that one big party was replaced by many small ones. The most notable of these proved to be the All-Russian Communist Party (Bolsheviks), headed by the consistent Stalinist Nina Andreeva, and the Russian Communist Workers' Party (RCWP), whose chief ideologist was Richard Kosolapov. The politics of the RCWP, which has undertaken one protest action after another, and which calls for a return to the traditional values of the pre-perestroika period, has attracted the support of the most deprived strata of society, but simultaneously alienated skilled workers and intellectuals. Joint activity with democratic socialists has proved impossible. This current organized a series of demonstrations in Moscow: on 9 February 1992, twenty thousand assembled to protest against price rises; on 23 February, a smaller gathering to commemorate those killed in the Second World War was brutally broken up by the police, attracting considerable public sympathy; and on 17 March, thirty thousand assembled in Manezh Square to insist that the Soviet Union still legally exists. While these dogmatic organizations can attract veteran grassroots Communists, they have no appeal for most young people and will not win the mass of citizens to their side. However, they are prepared to take to the streets, making life uncomfortable for the government – this marks them off from other former Communist currents.

The Socialist Workers' Party, founded by the former dissident Roy Medvedev on the basis of Gorbachev's last programme – which was to have been discussed at the Twenty-Ninth Congress of the CPSU – has attracted the support of several former Communist members of the Russian parliament and other former senior officials, but lacks a numerous and active membership. The small organizations, the Union of Communists and the United Communist Party, have even less chance of success.

For its part, the embryonic Party of Labour encountered all the difficulties that historically have confronted left-wing organizations in Russia. In the autumn of 1991, the political achievements of a majority of the left organizations in Russia looked far from impressive. After the Communist bureaucracy's domination of the mass media had been replaced by a liberal monopoly, the left found itself the only section among the former opposition to have gained nothing from the changes; indeed it had lost a great deal. The Socialist Party, the Anarcho-Syndicalists and the left opposition within the CPSU all proved to have adjusted badly to the new conditions. In spring 1991, the Second Congress of the Socialist Party had declared the need for a 'new opposition' and the 'politics of a third force'. These slogans were supported by the Anarcho-Syndicalists and the 'Greens'. The trouble was, however, that the 'third force' remained indecently weak.

Six months later, having failed to achieve the status of a 'third force', the democratic left nevertheless emerged as the sole hope for the opposition; yet it remained disorganized and demoralized by its lack of success. A split occurred among the Socialists, the catalyst of which was the founding of the Party of Labour. The moderate wing, headed by Mikhail Maliutin and Vladimir Lepekhin, sharply attacked the organizers of the Party of Labour, claiming that its designation as a class party was 'sectarian' and 'ultra-left'. In the opinion of this grouping, the only politics feasible in contemporary Russia, in the absence of a market, was 'not so much left-wing in spirit as left-liberal and, at best, social-democratic'.[5] Against the background of the failure of attempts to create social democracy in Russia and Eastern Europe, and in the absence of a civilized business class capable of becoming the bearer of 'enlightened liberalism', such utterances sounded quite empty, although they were symptomatic of the demoralization felt by many on the left during the perestroika period.

Collaboration with the trade unions radically changed the outlook of the left-wing activists. The CAS ideologist, Andrei Isaev, editor of the trade-union newspaper *Solidarnost*, turned it into an organ of the new opposition, and Party of Labour supporters in the Moscow and regional soviets were able to combine actions for workers' rights with defence of the principle of representative power. The unification of groups with varying ideological traditions – some of whom, in the past, had engaged in sharp polemics with each other – proceeded with surprising ease. Nevertheless, may differences remained unresolved. As might have been anticipated, the positions of the MFTU leadership and those of left-wing activists did not always coincide, particularly as the Party of Labour represented an influential opposition within the Moscow unions themselves. Shmakov and Nagaitseev had to deal with the consequences of their own doctrine insisting on the unions' political neutrality. Although intended primarily as a bulwark against control by the CPSU, in the new conditions the doctrine was deployed against the Party of Labour.[6]

Thus, despite unavoidable differences and conflicts, union leaders and the activists of radical groupings were able to work together. The organizational weakness of the left-wing groups forced them to depend on the unions even when a majority of the activists were unhappy with the decisions of union bosses. The latter, in turn, depended on the help of left-radical groups in their confrontation with the authorities. This difficult, contradictory, but essential collaboration once again revealed the weakness of both sides. In order to gain in strength and authority, the Party of Labour will require an increased level of activism and heightened political consciousness, the extension of democratic changes within the unions, as well as a higher level of organization, effectiveness and discipline among the former members of radical groups.

In the last analysis, the transformation of the Party of Labour into a unified and incipiently mass party depends on the degree to which the workers themselves and their families are drawn into politics. And this, in turn, places a great responsibility on the current leaderships of the party and the unions. The spontaneous protest of the population against the policies of Yeltsin and Gaidar may subsequently be reflected in a sharp rise in membership and support for the left-wing movement – or it may take the form of an uncontrolled revolt. It should be borne in mind that *all* political forces in Russia today are very weak in terms of membership as a result of the legacy of popular mistrust of political organization. This will test the capacity of the left – first and foremost the Party of Labour – and the unions to build a genuine and attractive alternative.

The Party of Labour, a majority of whose activists were never in the CPSU, is attractive to many precisely because it bears no responsibility for the past and is striving to find an alternative way forward. The published appeal that preceded its formation outlined a comprehensive programme that included a formal right to work and social guarantees, as well as increased workers' self-management and democratic control of the economy in the transition to a civilized market. The rights of women and national minorities would also be safeguarded.[7] However, the party's advantages are also its problems. While the party has the considerable advantage of not being burdened by a legacy of guilt, it lacks the links, structures and cadres of those organizations emerging from the core of the CPSU. It is natural, therefore, that despite the growing support of public opinion, the development of the Party of Labour – literally in a political vacuum – lags behind that of other parties.

The headlong collapse of the economy poses the question of the left's anti-crisis strategy at the practical level. Broad sectors of the public were initially disposed to see whether the government's measures could work. After all the incessant talk of markets and perestroika, Gaidar at least seemed to be taking an axe to the old system. And since the reforms had been long-heralded, many families had laid in stocks of the most essential items. But the patience of the people began to wear thin as the scale and sheer irresponsibility of the wrecking operation became clear. Consequently, a willingness to consider alternatives is growing. But there exists the problem of getting any message across to a broader public, since the media remain, for the most part, under the control or influence of the government, which, notwithstanding its *laissez faire* cant, uses its monopolistic position ruthlessly to keep the newspapers and broadcasting media in line.[8]

The left's task is to ensure that the public sector is not destroyed and looted, but rather rehabilitated as a driving force capable of pulling the country out of chaos. This requires establishing the most important priorities and concentrating social resources in them. It is possible, taking into account the experience of Western Keynesianism, to employ a policy of controlled inflation while not freeing prices altogether.[9] At the same time, it would be essential to create the conditions for the growth of independent enterprises 'from below', protecting them from being smothered by the monopolies and from collapse in conditions of economic chaos. These are, however, suspect 'socialist' measures that were successfully employed in the West during the Great Depression. One other condition is, however, necessary for their success: an increase in the political weight of the workers' organizations, trade unions and left parties – those forces capable of realizing such a programme or of controlling its implementation from below. While this condition does not exist, the hopes for some sort of Russian 'New Deal', and consequently for overcoming the crisis, will remain illusory.

Notes

1. Of course the decay of the statocracy into a variety of regional and bureaucratic fiefdoms has a historical specificity of its own. I have analysed the old Soviet statocracy in *The Thinking Reed*, London 1988. It is interesting to note that the learned Marx scholar Eero Loone happily refers to the 'feudal' features of the Soviet social formation in *Soviet Marxism and Analytic Philosophies of History*, London and Moscow 1992, p. 219 et seq.

2. *Kommersant*, no. 47, 1991, p. 1.

3. See Giovanni Arrighi, 'World Income Inequalities', NLR 189, September–October 1991.

4. See Stanislav Menshikov, *Catharsis or Catastrophe: the Soviet Economy Today*, Moscow and London 1991, p. 13.
5. O Grigorev, V. Lepekhin, M. Maliutin, 'Partia truda v sovremennoi Rossii: neobkhodimost' i vozmozhnost'', Moscow 1991, p. 63.
6. *Solidarnost*, no. 16, 1991, p. 4.
7. See *Obozrevatel*, special issue, January 1992.
8. In February 1992 I received my first invitation to write for *Pravda*, a critique of the economic reform published on 14 February, but this paper, if it does not close for good, may only be able to survive thanks to government help.
9. For the elements of a post-Soviet 'Keynesian' economics see Menshikov, *Catharsis or Catastrophe?*